Rural Church
RESCUE:

A Call to Restore Healthy Churches to Rural North America

Jon Sanders

THANK YOU!

To the reader: Before you even begin reading this book, I just
want to say thank you from the bottom of my heart. I really
mean that. Writing this book has been one of the most
difficult projects I have ever undertaken. Not only is it a lot of
work to put content down in writing in a way that doesn't
completely abuse the English language and is understandable
for others to follow along with, but it has also been a pretty
daunting challenge to be vulnerable and put my thoughts and
ideas out there for others to either approve or condemn,
applaud or criticize, accept or reject. Ultimately my prayer all
along has been that God would use this book to encourage,
inform, inspire, and challenge pastors and leaders in the small-
town and rural setting. Regardless of whether or not you agree
with everything you will read in the pages to follow, I'm
grateful that you are choosing to join me for the journey. I
pray your leadership and ministry will be better off in some
way because of it.

I also want to say a huge thank you to my awesome wife
Jessica and my kids Justin, Jennifer, and James for continually
sticking by my side and supporting me in ministry. I could not
and would not be where I am today without you. I love you
all!

Finally, I want to thank my spiritual family at The RESCUE
Church. To all who have been a part of the journey over the
years and have served alongside me, thank you! I am so
thankful for the privilege of being your pastor. I have truly
loved the adventure of the past 15 years and I look forward to
many more, Lord willing. Thank you for letting me share
some of our story with other pastors and church leaders.

CONTENTS

Introduction: Imagine   i

Part One: My Story   1

Chapter 1: Dream Job   2

Chapter 2: Do What?   5

Chapter 3: If God Can Speak Through a Jackass   8

Part Two: God's Fire & Rescue   13

Chapter 4: Recognize the Mission   15

Chapter 5: Execute Strong Leadership   23

Chapter 6: Speak a Compelling Vision   34

Chapter 7: Cover the Community   51

Chapter 8: Unleash the Volunteers   80

Chapter 9: Embrace the Future...But Honor the Past   101

Conclusion   113

Appendix A: Can Multi-Site Work in a Rural Context?   116

Imagine...

Imagine the following scenario with me for just a moment...

Today is just another routine, ordinary day in your city. Things are going along as they always do, business as usual. But all of a sudden the tranquil normalcy of the day is obliterated as an epic explosion rocks your community. In an instant several city blocks have been entirely leveled leaving only smoldering piles of debris where houses stood just seconds before. All around the parameter of the blast zone homes and businesses are burning. Many people died instantly while countless others are in imminent danger. People are trapped...wounded...unresponsive...dying. From every direction the desperate screams for help and rescue can be heard.

Within seconds of the explosion, you and many others are reaching for your cell phones and dialing the three-digit number that everyone knows to call in emergency situations...9-1-1. You are desperate for the rapid life-saving response of skilled fire fighters, paramedics, and police officers. They are greatly needed...and they are needed *RIGHT NOW!*

Although it feels like an eternity, you soon hear the sounds of sirens making their way through your city to the scene of carnage and chaos. Help has arrived. Lives will be saved. Order will be restored.

Or...so you thought.

But as the responding rescue units begin arriving on scene you can't believe what you are hearing and seeing. Because the incident is so massive in scale, it requires multiple EMS agencies from all around the region to be dispatched. As the rescuers begin to assemble and survey the situation, it becomes immediately obvious they are adding more confusion and pandemonium to an already chaotic situation.

You notice that there seems to be a lot of competition and animosity between the various fire departments. Instead of working together to rescue trapped and injured people, they are spending more time criticizing and putting down the other fire departments' approaches, styles, and techniques.

And as bad as the fire departments seem to despise each other, you notice even *more* bickering and infighting within each individual rescue unit. You wonder how people who seem to dislike each other so much will possibly ever be able to work together as a cohesive unit to perform the rescue operations that seem to be going completely unnoticed.

As you look on in stunned amazement, you also notice that no one can agree on any form of leadership structure or how decisions will be made or *who* will make them. Instead of the rescuers jumping headlong into the much needed rescue efforts under the vision and leadership of a qualified chief, they are having a makeshift business meeting on the spot, voting to elect the various committees who will be responsible for making decisions about the rescue operation.

It seems one of the biggest concerns on everyone's mind is how much money a rescue operation of this magnitude will cost. And to your shock you listen in as the various rescue agencies delay responding to the needs of others while they sort out who will pay for all the man power, supplies, and wear and tear on equipment.

As you move about from one group of responders to the next you can overhear various members of the rescue teams starting to argue about whether or not the trapped victims were predestined to be in that situation or if it was a result of their own poor decisions.

You hear others voicing complaints about the style or volume of music that is coming from the radio on the ambulance down the street. Other rescuers are choosing to disassociate with one another because they don't care for how the other departments are dressed. They are obviously disgusted with one another's choices in bunker gear and uniforms.

After all of this you *finally* notice some rescuers beginning to get about the business of engaging the actual situation. But upon further observation, you're shocked when you realize that they are beginning to put their focus on restoring the destroyed *buildings and houses* instead of responding to the screams for help coming from *people* trapped within the many piles of rubble.

As if all of this hasn't been bad enough, your breaking point comes at about exactly 60 minutes past the arrival of the first rescue unit on scene. In utter disbelief, you watch as one responder after another begins to 'call it a day' and walk off the scene. They reason that no one should have to put in more than one hour of service on any given week. After all, they don't want to be viewed as one of those "crazy, radical types" who gives way too much of themselves to all this rescue stuff. So they plan to be back to give another 60 minutes of their "service" next week...probably...if the weather isn't too bad...or too good either for that matter...because they might have to try out that new set of golf clubs they recently purchased.

If the above hypothetical situation ever really played out like that in the EMS world, people would be OUTRAGED! The story would break on every national media outlet and all the talking heads would be calling it an 'abdication of duty'. Public outcry would be deafening, as people across the nation demanded the firing and even possible criminal charges for the department heads along with every other rescue personnel involved.

However, when the above hypothetical situation plays itself out in very similar and not-so-hypothetical ways every single day in the church world...we just call it...well...*church*!

In a world that has been absolutely devastated by the destructive force of sin...when people all around us are crying out to be rescued...when the fires of hell consume more and more lost souls every day...when the life-saving gospel of Jesus Christ and the rapid response from his church who has been commissioned with the task of rescuing others from the flames is so greatly needed...the church largely seems to be floundering.

- Countless churches are aimlessly adrift due to a severe lack of God-called leaders and a biblical leadership structure that empowers those leaders to offer the very thing God has put in their hearts as a gift to the church... *leadership*.

- And without strong, healthy, God-ordained leadership, many churches are also lacking a God-inspired vision for reaching their communities for Christ. When a church ceases to have a vision from God that keeps their focus outward, it's only a matter of time before they become inwardly focused, not only on their own personal comfort, but also focusing their battles and fighting *within* the church, against each other, instead of against the real enemy.

- Church leaders and church attendees subscribe to an unhealthy belief that the church down the street with a different denominational title or slightly different doctrinal statement is a greater threat to their mission rather than the forces of spiritual evil and darkness that are blinding countless lost souls from the truth.

- Churches seem to be so resistant to anything that resembles change or progress. It's as if the focus has been shifted away from being a rescue mission to that of a preservation mission! *"Avoid and resist change at all cost"*, has become the mission statement of so many stagnant and dying churches.

- Churches are more concerned with the numbers of dollars in their savings account than the number of lost souls in their communities! Many of these churches piously say things like, "Oh, we're not into the numbers," as a way of excusing their lack of spiritual and attendance growth, but they will wage a passionate war on anyone who would suggest diverting some of the "numbers" from the budget to go into community outreach. Rather than trusting God to provide for the very mission He's called them to, they seek to protect their assets that will allow them to keep their doors open and their traditions alive for many generations to come. They really do care about numbers...just not the numbers *God* cares about.

- Christians seem to be preoccupied with arguing and dividing over doctrinal issues, ministry philosophies, strategies, methodology, and styles instead of focusing our unified efforts on the great rescue mission at hand.

- Many churches are putting a higher value on their facilities and buildings than on reaching people to gather as the *real* church within those buildings. Sadly for too many people, the church IS the building.

And as dismal as all of this is, it gets worse. For many churches are so stuck in stagnant decay that they rarely realize the extent of their problems. These churches yawn and continue their slumber, waking up only occasionally to protect and defend the status quo in order to maintain the time-honored traditions of "the way we've always done it". And as a result, our world no longer even looks to the church as a relevant source of rescue or help. In many cases, the church has become largely inconsequential in the lives of a community and its citizens.

If you think I'm overstating my case, let me ask you to consider this: What do you suppose would happen if we approached the city council or authorities that govern your city or town and proposed that we shut down one or more of the local fire stations? People would speak up...and loudly. Meetings would be held. Petitions would be signed. The decision would not be popular or go down without some major opposition. Why? Because most people realize the vital mission the fire department upholds and the value it adds to its community. And yet every year, all across the nation, churches are closing their doors and fading out of their communities and no one seems to even notice or care. It seems that the general public no longer recognizes the vital mission that the church has been called to or realizes any real value the church adds to the community.

But I believe there is hope. It doesn't have to be this way. And thankfully, for the far-too-many Christians who are currently experiencing this in their own churches, it doesn't have to *stay* this way. In the pages ahead I want to do more than simply expose what's wrong with the church (anyone can do that). I want to offer some very practical, simple, and biblical **solutions** to the problems that are plaguing so much of the church today. I want to help you not only believe God for greater things in your church, but help point you down the path to actually seeing it happen. But I must warn you up front. Just

because a solution may be *simple* doesn't make it *easy*.
And just because a solution is practical doesn't mean it
won't require radical courage to implement. And just
because a solution is biblical doesn't mean it will be
politically correct and liked by everyone. But if you long
to see the church…your church…once again embrace the
vision of RESCUE that Jesus called it to…if you long to
be a part of something that is bigger than yourself and
will outlive your life and last for all eternity…then I invite
you to take this journey with me. Keep reading!

If I've already offended you with what I've written so far,
you will probably want do yourself a favor and put this
book down right now. There's no way you're ready for
what lies ahead. Go back to your peaceful, religious
slumber. We can get to know and appreciate each other
more in heaven (probably), but for now…I've got some
fires to fight and a rescue mission to join Jesus in!

PART ONE:

MY STORY

I'm sure you didn't necessarily pick up this book to learn a lot about *me* and *my life*. Ultimately, my desire in writing this book is to help build Christ's eternal kingdom by challenging and inspiring Christ-followers to step into the eternal rescue mission that Jesus has called us to. I want this book to be about *you* and how God desires to use *your life* for His purposes. Having said that however, I believe in order for you to join me on this journey, it might be helpful for you to know a little about who I am and how God has worked in and through my life to teach me the insights that I will share in this book. So humor me for just a few pages as I share my testimony.

CHAPTER 1

DREAM JOB

I didn't pay attention to the actual time the alarm clock announced with its glowing red numbers as it sat on the nightstand next to my bed. My mind simply knew it was not yet time to wake up. My body agreed. But the abrasive tones that shattered the dark silence of Peoria's Fire Station 11 in the middle of that winter night said otherwise. I forced myself to focus as the calm female voice of the 911 dispatcher immediately followed the tones with the address and description of the emergency…*a structure fire!* Within seconds, the tranquility of the firehouse sleeping quarters was transformed into a flurry of activity as I, along with the rest of the crew of Engine 11 quickly got dressed and headed out to the apparatus bay. Even though we were all tired and sore having just returned from yet another house fire less than two hours earlier, our crew jumped into our still-wet bunker gear, onto the fire engine, and out the door. In less than 3 minutes, we had gone from being sound asleep in the comfort of our warm beds to wide awake, hearts pumping, adrenaline rushing, as we were now racing down the mostly deserted Peoria streets with our lights and sirens clearing what little traffic remained out of our way. In the back seat of Engine 11 I was quickly strapping on my air pack and making the final preparations to my gear and assembling the tools I would need so that I would be ready to step off the fire engine and move quickly inside the burning structure if and when directed by my captain to do so. As we turned onto the street we had been dispatched to, we could immediately see the dancing, yellow glow that lit up a good part of the block. My captain began to give a report over the radio to the other engine companies, truck companies, rescue units, and battalion chief that were still in route: "Engine 11 is on scene. We've got a two-story, single-family occupancy with heavy fire showing from the garage. Engine 11 will be making the attack. Engine 16, catch a hydrant on the way in." As our rig came to a stop our crew jumped into action. While the traumatized family, whose home we were there to save, along with a handful of concerned neighbors looked on, the men and women of The Peoria Fire Department got down to the business of doing what firefighters do...*saving lives and protecting property.* Myself and a few others made our way through the smoke-filled house to attack the fire and battle it back toward the garage where it had started, thus saving the rest of the home from destruction. At the same time the rest of our team outside the house were busy securing permanent water supply from nearby hydrants, opening up the roof to ventilate the smoke from the garage, protecting the neighboring structures from catching on fire, and working to support the efforts of myself and the other guys who were fighting the fire on the inside. In short order the fire was put out. We had contained the damage primarily to the garage. We saved the home. We saved the neighbors home. We had restored order and calm to the panic-stricken scene of chaos that we had rolled up on just 20 minutes prior.

I will never forget the overwhelming sense of purpose and satisfaction I felt that night, as I had so many other times before. My heart was full of gratitude that God would allow me to be a part of a team that was called to a mission that was so much bigger than *myself!* The thought that I got to work along side such brave and honorable guys to do a job that I loved so much warmed my soul on that frigid night. I can remember sitting on top of a fire engine helping fold the frozen supply line back into the hose bed, looking around at all of "my guys" in our ice-covered gear with icicles hanging from the rims of our helmets and saying these words out loud, "Man, I *LOVE* my job!"

Little did I know on that night that God would soon be asking me to leave this job that I loved so dearly. As much as I loved the danger and adventure and gratifying work of saving lives and protecting property that the fire service provided, I would soon discover a calling from God to step into an even greater adventure that would come with a cost of incredible risk and sacrifice. A calling to fight the eternal flames of hell and be used by God to rescue not just physical lives, but eternal souls. Everything was about to change...or was it *really?*

CHAPTER 2
DO WHAT?
MY CALL TO MINISTRY

Confession. I never wanted to be a pastor. Even though I grew up in a pastor's home and truly loved the church, and even though I had committed my life to Christ at a young age, and even though I had promised to follow the Lord's will for my life regardless of where that might lead me, I had bigger aspirations for my life than pastoral ministry.

To be completely honest, as a young kid and even into my teenage years my career goal was to grow up and play professional football for the Minnesota Vikings. (They must have lost my phone number at some point because as of this writing, they *still* haven't called to offer me a position!) So as I entered my high school years, reality began to suggest that I might want to have a back up career plan just in case the whole NFL thing didn't pan out.

As a kid, I had always been attracted to the lights and sirens of fire trucks and the rush of adrenaline those guys had to be experiencing as they raced down the road to an emergency call. So as a sophomore in high school I decided that I was going to be a fire fighter for the City of Peoria, IL.

As a sophomore in high school I also made another major life decision…I was going to marry Jessica Vogel as soon as I possibly could. (Growing up, my Dad had

always told me to *"marry my best friend someday."* As a
young child, this never made much sense to me because I
had no desire to spend the rest of my life with my best
friend, Jeff Harriman as my wife! But when I met Jessica
and we began dating in our teen years, she quickly
became my best friend and Dad's words started to make
much more sense to me! I knew I would spend the rest
of my life with her.)

To have my entire life mapped out by the age of 15 felt
pretty good! I would marry Jessica, get a degree in Fire
Science from Illinois Central College, get hired on the
Peoria Fire Department, and live happily ever after! And
so I set about the business of making that happen. With
the support of both of our parents, Jessica and I were
married in November of my senior year of high school.
We purposefully bought our first home in a small
community outside of the city of Peoria because it had a
volunteer fire department that I could get involved with
to begin gaining experience for the career that I was
pursuing. The fall after I graduated from high school I
began taking my college courses for a degree in Fire
Science. And within three years of leaving high school,
by God's grace I was hired as a fire fighter with the City
of Peoria. I love it when a plan comes together!

But sometimes God has different plans than ours. Has
God ever messed up your plans? If so, I can totally relate
because that's exactly what He did to *my* plans! As I've
already mentioned, I was loving life as a fire fighter. God
had blessed us with two children, a nice house, nice
vehicles, and a black lab. We were well on our way to the
"happily ever after" part of my plan…except for this *one*
thing.

From the time I was in junior high, I had a pretty good sense that God wanted to use my life in some form of pastoral ministry. Before I married Jessica, I made sure that she was good with that 'JUST IN CASE' God would ever come calling, but I assured her that the chances of that happening were very slim! But in my quiet moments…when it was just me and God…when I allowed myself to listen to His voice…the call to ministry was an ever-present whisper in my life. It was a whisper that I tried to stifle many times. It was something that I truly tried to run from. But as the years went on the whisper grew in frequency and volume and I *knew* deep in my soul that God was calling me to something even bigger than the fire service that I so deeply loved. I wrestled with the call to full-time pastoral ministry because I knew the implications would mean leaving a job that I had worked so hard to obtain and following God into a very uncertain future.

But in the summer of 2002, in spite of all my running and suppressing and stifling, I finally yielded to the gentle, but constant whisper of God's call upon my life to ministry. I said YES to serving God completely with my life…even if that meant leaving the fire service and going who-knows-where to be a pastor. Even though I felt as if a huge burden had been lifted from my shoulders when I finally surrendered to God's call, I was still very uncertain that He had chosen the right guy to be used by Him for anything of eternal significance and I was about to throw out some serious arguments to the Lord as to exactly why His choosing *me* for ministry was a bad idea!

CHAPTER 3

IF GOD CAN SPEAK THROUGH A JACKASS

GOD BUILT HIS CHURCH IN SPITE OF ME

Have you ever read the account of Moses arguing with God when God gave him the assignment to go speak to Pharaoh and demand that he release the children of Israel from captivity (Exodus 3-4)? Well I had several similar conversations with the Lord in the aftermath of my surrender to pastoral ministry. I threw up many different problems that I was quite sure God hadn't considered when He called me to be a pastor. So I took it upon myself to point out some of these realities to God. Things such as:

- "I'm not old enough to be a pastor." (I was only 23 years old at the time.)
- "I'm not experienced enough to be a pastor."
- "I'm not educated enough to be a pastor."
- "I'm not smart enough to be a pastor."
- "I'm not skilled enough to be a pastor."
- "I don't have enough financial resources to move my family somewhere and start a church from scratch."

But that summer, God's voice seemed to cut right through the clutter of my excuses and self-proclaimed limitations. One verse that God used to radically impact my life at this time was 2 Chronicles 16:9a which says, *"For the eyes of the Lord move to and fro throughout the earth that He may strongly support those whose heart is completely His."* (NASB) Essentially this says that God is searching the globe at any given moment, looking for a man or woman whom He may *"strongly support"*. When I think about what it must look like to be strongly supported by the very God who created the heavens and the earth, that sounds like something I'd like to get in on. But according to that verse, the one condition that must be met, the ingredient that God is searching for in a man or woman is that their heart must be completely His.

During the summer of 2002 God used this verse to say to me, *"I don't need you to be old enough or experienced enough or smart enough in order for me to use you. I need you to be OBEDIENT enough and willing to follow me. I want to use your life to demonstrate that it's not about what you bring to the table, but about what I can do through the life of an individual that is submitted to my authority and leadership."* Even though I'm pretty good at arguing, it was hard to combat that logic. Essentially God was saying that if I was willing to obey and do my part, He was willing to be God and do His part. So my family and I began to prepare to leave the fire service and become church planters.

While there are so many lessons that God taught us during this time, and so many cool "God stories" I could share from this season of our lives, in order to keep this section brief, let me give you a condensed overview of

9

God's faithfulness to make good on His promise to use me in pastoral ministry:

- God led Jessica and I very clearly to plant a church in the rural community of Flandreau, South Dakota. (The story of how we had this connection is a long one worth another book of its own!)
- In April 2004 we said goodbye to our families and the Peoria Fire Department and moved to Flandreau to begin the work of planting a church.
- Even though we had very limited resources and extremely humble beginnings, God began to grow a church. We first started in a small rented community center-type space. Then we moved our services into an elementary school. And eventually, God provided us with a more permanent facility of our own.
- In 2009 God gave me a very clear vision of using technology to reproduce our church into rural communities all across the Midwest. Even though I had never heard the term *multi-site* church planting, I soon learned that this is exactly what God was calling us to. A multi-site church can be defined as one church that meets in multiple locations that share the same leadership, vision, DNA, and budget.
- As of this writing, The RESCUE Church has grown to three campuses in South Dakota, Illinois, and Jamaica as well as an online iCampus that features LIVE weekly broadcasts of our worship services and has a growing audience of people all over the United States and around the

world. You can learn more about our church and our story on our website at www.therescuechurch.com

- In the last ten years of pastoral ministry, we have seen God use us in ways beyond anything we could have ever imagined. There are souls who will spend eternity in heaven because of how Jesus Christ used our lives to impact others. In addition to seeing souls saved, we have seen marriages healed, addictions overcome, and broken lives restored!

I don't write about the successes of our ministry to point any glory in our direction. I'm simply making the point that I have experienced first-hand the ability of God to deliver on His promise to do extraordinary things for His kingdom through ordinary people who are willing to sign up for the ride. And along the way, God has also taught me valuable lessons that I believe He wants me to pass on to others. Not only has He opened my eyes to some of the major problems that are plaguing the rural church today, I believe He has also given me some insight into how to overcome some of those issues.

And for me, the unique way God has opened my eyes to all of this is through the lens of the fire service. You see, I thought He was telling me to leave my profession as a fire fighter when He called me into ministry. But what I have come to learn is that He was simply calling me into a different type of firefighting! And He has used my involvement with fighting physical fires to teach me some very real metaphors when it comes to the church's mission to fight the eternal fires of hell.

If you'd like to know some of these insights keep reading...

PART TWO:

GOD'S FIRE & RESCUE

Having spent years in the fire service, both paid and volunteer, and having spent more than a decade in church planting, pastoring, and full-time vocational ministry, I've come to realize some major similarities in the mission of the Church and the fire department. My prayer is that through highlighting these similarities I can offer a reminder to Christ-followers what it is we've been called to as well as give some tangible solutions to the church who feels as though they are stuck and in need of some inspiration and direction. I would contend that the fire service has a thing or two it can teach (or remind) the church.

In the chapters to follow, I will outline these lessons using the acronym R-E-S-C-U-E. I believe that if a church embraces the 6 principles of RESCUE, they will be well on the way to reclaiming the vital role that God has called them to in their community.

- **R**ecognize the mission
- **E**xecute strong leadership
- **S**peak a compelling vision
- **C**over the community
- **U**nleash the volunteers
- **E**mbrace the future...but still honor the past

DISCLAIMER: Before we go any further, I do just want to speak a word of caution not to view these principles as a 6-step *formula* or *model* for church growth or "success". While I believe every one of these are extremely important, the reality is Jesus Christ is the one who has promised to build *his* church through the power of the Holy Spirit. So to be clear, I'm not saying that if a church does these following things apart from Christ's supernatural power they should expect any success. I challenge you to prayerfully apply these principles to your church under submission to the authority and ownership of Jesus.

Let's get started…

CHAPTER 4

RECOGNIZE THE MISSION

The fire service knows its mission...

One thing that sets the fire service apart from so many other organizations in the world today is that its members are crystal clear on what their purpose and calling is. Ask any fire fighter why their fire department exists and what it is they are supposed to be doing and you will likely hear the reply, *"we exist to save lives and protect property."* Ask the average Christian, or pastor for that matter, why their church exists and you're likely to get a far less clear response. It seems somewhere along the way many in the church have failed to remember why the church exists in the first place or what it is we're supposed to be about the business of doing. But it doesn't have to be this way. Jesus Christ, the head of the church (Colossians 1:18) has given us very clear direction and insight into what is near and dear to his heart.

- Luke 19:10 "For the Son of Man came to **seek** and to **save** the lost." When I hear the phrase *"seek and save"* I also hear *"search and rescue"*.

- Jude 1:23 "Save others by snatching them from the fire..."

15

- Matthew 28:19-20 "Go and make disciples of all nations, baptizing them in the name of the Father and of the Son and of the Holy Spirit, and teaching them to obey everything I have commanded you…"

- Mark 16:15 "Go into all the world and preach the gospel to all creation."

The Bible makes it clear that we have been called to join Jesus in *his* mission of seeking and saving lost people through the presentation and promotion of the gospel. In his time spent here on earth, Jesus spoke more about the reality of hell than he did heaven. It's almost as if Jesus believed that hell is real and eternal and that he did not desire that anyone should go there. He was clear on his mission and why he had come to earth. And he has not been unclear with his command to his church as to what our mission is either.

Yet sadly, there are many churches today that have drifted so far from the mission that Christ has called them to. I can't tell you how many times I have had someone approach me after a service and say something like, "I've sat in church my entire life and I've never heard that message before." What message you ask? The gospel. That's it. The simple truth that Jesus died to take our sin upon himself and rose victoriously from the grave defeating sin and death and hell and that in order to be restored back into a right relationship with the Father in heaven, I must put my full faith and trust in the name of Jesus Christ. Many churches have lost sight of the centrality of the gospel and as a result they are not experiencing much of God's blessing and power in their efforts.

Imagine a fire department responding to the scene of a house fire where people have been badly burned and have sustained life-threatening injuries. Now imagine that as the firefighters arrive they make it a priority to tell the victims which political candidate will best reflect the values of their department and thus help support their continued existence. Or what if they offered food for anyone who might be hungry on the scene? Or maybe they showed up with chicken dinners and baked goods for sale in hopes that the victims and bystanders at the scene might help contribute toward some of the financial burdens that the fire department faces. Imagine that they offered these poor victims everything *except* life-saving water to extinguish the flames and medical help that they so desperately need. The end result would be that the house would burn to the ground and the people would die because their greatest need of rescue was not met.

This is exactly what is happening in so many churches in our land today. People show up week after week with their spiritual lives on fire and in need of the life-saving "water" and "medical attention" of the gospel. But instead of providing the gospel, the church offers up a political agenda, a social justice program, a fund raising opportunity, a sports activity, a quilting bee in the church basement, busyness and activities that have a "form of godliness" (2 Timothy 3:5), but lack the eternal life-saving power of the gospel.

It's high time that the church of Jesus Christ returns to her first priority and makes the salvation of lost souls paramount to everything else! A fire department that doesn't save lives and protect property is no fire department at all! Likewise, a church that is not involved in Christ's mission of seeking and saving lost souls is no church at all!

The fire service embraces messy people and chaotic situations...

I need to offer up a warning at this point in the conversation. Many Christians *say* they're excited about their church reaching people for Jesus...until their church starts reaching people for Jesus! You know why? Because reaching people for Jesus is a messy and costly business! And unless the people of the church are clear on the mission of the church they will shy away from the messy business of reaching people with the gospel. They will act surprised, maybe even disapproving, when messy, broken, "sinners" walk through their doors. In that moment, instead of seeing a soul in desperate need of rescue, the church will see an outsider, an outcast, an inconvenience, and will treat them accordingly. And before long at all, the broken, hurting, lost sinners will stop coming to the church altogether, leaving only the deceived and disobedient professing Christ-followers to maintain their weekly gatherings and rituals that might make them *look* like a church on the outward appearance even though they are failing to fulfill their most basic mission.

The fire department, on the other hand, *embraces* messy, chaotic situations. Instead of shying away from broken and hurting people in need, they rush toward them. Why? One reason. They know why they exist. They are clear on their sole purpose of "saving lives and protecting property." This is why they stand ready at any given moment to drop whatever it is they're doing and move toward messy and chaotic situations. They fully expect that when they pull up on the scene of a fire or vehicle crash or medical emergency they will encounter difficult situations with difficult people. They know they are going to have to see things they really don't want to see. They accept the reality that the only reason they were called to the scene in the first place is because someone *needed* something from them. This puts them in the role of the givers, the providers, and the rescuers. They expect nothing from the people they serve and are prepared to give them everything, even their lives if needed.

I believe this is exactly what Christ envisions for his church! In Matthew 9:11, Jesus' disciples were confronted by the Pharisees (the religious establishment) with the question of why Jesus chose to hang out with "*those* people" (tax collectors, prostitutes, sinners). I love Jesus' response to that crowd of self-righteous religious leaders. He told them, "It is not the healthy who need a doctor, but the sick. But go and learn what this means: 'I desire mercy, not sacrifice.' *For I have not come to call the righteous, but sinners.*" (Matthew 9:12-13) Don't miss this. In this passage we see Jesus declare in no uncertain terms why he came to this earth...to engage, interact with, and reach out to sick people. Sinners. The mission of Jesus Christ does not focus on religious people who do a good job of keeping rules and defending tradition. Jesus is all about rescuing sinners. Period.

Jon Sanders

This passage of Scripture has become the inspiration behind a powerful statement that our church adopted a few years ago. While we were not the ones to come up with this statement (I don't know whom to credit with the original quote.), it goes like this:

"This church is not a memorial for saints, but a hospital for sinners."

We have this statement on our signs outside each one of our campuses, on the backs of hundreds of T-shirts that our people have worn all over our communities and even around the world, on our website, our social media and just about anywhere else we can think to put it. Why? Because we want everyone to know that our church does not exist as a memorial or museum for the saints (That means us, by the way. The New Testament calls Christians *saints.*), but that we exist to be a place where broken people in need of healing and relief and rescue will be welcomed and accepted. In other words, this church does not exist primarily for us, but for those who are still in need of rescue.

So how do you know if your church is in line with Christ's mission? Let me offer a few diagnostic questions:
1. Is the gospel message presented passionately and clearly on a weekly basis?
2. Are people being saved?
3. Are people being baptized?
4. Are people being rescued from destructive lifestyles and walking in freedom as growing Christ-followers?

5. Are new people coming through your doors on a regular basis?
6. Do guests feel accepted and welcomed?
7. Is your church outward focused?

If you can honestly answer these questions in the affirmative, then congratulations! Your church is walking in step with the true mission that Christ has called us to. Keep it up! But, if after careful consideration you would have to honestly admit that you rarely (if ever) see these things taking place in your church, that should be a clear indicator that somewhere along the way your church has drifted off course and is no longer living out the mission that Christ intends for his church. You need to get back on track! And to do this, your church is going to need strong pastoral leadership, which happens to be covered in the next chapter.

But before we move on to that chapter, I want to address an issue that fits really well at this point in the conversation.

What if God called you to pastor in a rural community...and He's asking you to _STAY_ in that rural community?

Most of us don't have a hard time recognizing the mission of the church. We get it. And we're even willing to engage in that mission in a rural context...for a while...at least to get some experience...you know...to put in our time and pay our dues...while we wait and hope for an opportunity to present itself somewhere else...somewhere other than here...somewhere in a bigger city where our work will really matter.

But what if rural really *did* matter? What if the people in rural places were an overlooked people group with significant problems and God was raising up a generation of leaders willing to go engage the mission of the cross in that context for a lifetime? What if you are one of those leaders? What if God wasn't going to call you onto to "bigger and better"? What if God wanted to use your life and leadership to make a big impact in a small place for eternity?

Getting back to my fire metaphor, let me ask you a question. Which context is better to save a life in, rural or urban? It's a dumb question, isn't it? Saving a life from fire is a noble task regardless of the size of city in which the rescue takes place!

So why is it that when it comes to rescuing people with the gospel, we've bought into the subtle lies that tell us it's more noble and honorable to engage in the mission of the church in a big city or the suburbs, but to be involved in the very same mission in a small-town or rural context is to somehow have been demoted to the penalty box? Pastor, if God has called you to serve Him in a small place, that is not synonymous with being called to a small, insignificant work! Your kingdom efforts in rural North America are desperately needed and completely noble. I want to challenge you to consider investing your entire tenure as a pastor in one place...a place that matters...a small place with huge opportunity to rescue souls for eternity!

CHAPTER 5

Execute Strong Leadership

The fire service has a clearly defined leadership structure...

I have had the honor to get to be a part of four different fire departments in my life (two full-time career departments and two volunteer departments). And I can tell you that with each one I never had to 'scratch my head' in wonder or try hard to figure out who was in charge and how decisions were made and carried out. The fire service subscribes to a very clear and defined leadership structure in which leaders make decisions to lead the fire department, both on and off the fire ground, and the rest of the membership submits to and follows that leadership. This leadership structure is absolutely vital in the chaotic environments of emergency scenes. When lives are on the line, when every second matters, what is needed most in those moments are clear and direct orders by gifted and capable leaders that will be carried out swiftly and completely by gifted and capable subordinates. The scene of a fire or other life-threatening emergency is neither the time nor the place to have discussions, debates, or committee meetings followed by voting with the outcome being determined by the 51% majority. Instead, the fire department recognizes the need for a qualified Incident Commander to assume command of the entire operation. As they offer leadership and direction, other leaders step into their roles to carry out the commands from the highest chief on the scene all the way down to the lowest firefighter. It's not about one person being "better" or "more important" than another. It's not a statement about who brings more value to the organization. It's about a flow of authority that results in many individual parts coming together and acting as one cohesive unit to accomplish the mission at hand.

Without strong leadership, fire ground operations would quickly become a chaotic circus. People would be hurt. Lives would be lost. The mission would suffer.

I am here to contend that much of the church in our world today is experiencing a leadership crisis. Instead of embracing the biblical model of church leadership in which leaders who have been called by God step up and lead the church, somewhere along the line we've adopted a structure of leadership that looks and smells a whole lot like the United States Federal Government (and we all know how smoothly and efficiently that operates!). Instead of pastors offering strong leadership to their congregations, we see churches that make most of their decisions based on committees posturing for power, business meetings, and votes. Whoever can leverage the most influence and gain the majority of the votes of the congregation calls the shots and sets the direction. Sadly in many churches, just because someone may have the title of *pastor* does not necessarily mean that they are the *leader*. I believe there are pastors who know that their churches have drifted off course and have strayed far outside of the mission that Christ has called his church to engage in. And even though they would *like* to see their churches return to the God-ordained purpose that Christ calls all churches to, they simply don't have the *permission* to lead their congregation back on track.

Prophet or Prostitute?

Sadly, many church members (and many pastors as well) have a very flawed view of the pastor's role as it pertains to leadership. They believe that since they *hired* the pastor, then in some practical way he *belongs* to the board or the congregation. Essentially, they get to dictate what he says from the pulpit and the vision he casts for the congregation. If they like it and approve of it, they'll go along with it. But the minute their hired-man steps out of line, they are there to remind him of who signs his paychecks and to whom he answers to. In a healthy church however, a strong lead pastor recognizes that while the church may have *hired* him, it is God who has *called* him and he ultimately answers to God for the messages he preaches, the vision he casts, and the direction he leads the church in. Now this is not to say that a senior pastor should not have authentic accountability in his life. He should. I firmly believe that a healthy leader surrounds himself with other strong leaders who do not think exactly the way he thinks and allows himself to be known in a very real way by his inner circle of leaders and friends. He has people in his life who have permission and a duty to call him out on sin in his life or any other warning signs that he is heading down a dangerous path. But with that healthy accountability in place, he clearly recognizes his call from God to lead the church as God directs.

I once heard a pastor friend of mine challenge a group of pastors at a church leadership conference with these words: "Pastor, you are either a prostitute or a prophet. A prostitute renders services for an agreed upon price; a prophet delivers a word from the Lord regardless of the price it may cost him!"

When we look into the New Testament and study the life of the early church, we don't see committees being formed or votes being taken. We don't see the direction of the church being set by whoever could come up with 51% of the votes. We don't see people hashing out decisions using *Robert's Rules of Order* and the art of Parliamentary procedure. Instead we see God-called leaders leading. We see God directing the course of the church through the visions he placed in the hearts of its apostles and pastors.

But if your church upbringing was anything like mine, most likely this was not the kind of leadership that was modeled for you. You can probably remember sitting through some long, boring, and at times fiery business meetings where church decisions were made. You quite possibly recall the pastor having some role in the meeting, but coming off as very weak and at the mercy of however 'we the people' voted. And even though this form of church government is found *nowhere* in Scripture, it can be found in a majority of churches (at least in the United States where we value our right to vote). So while not a *biblical* approach to church leadership, it's at least a *normal* approach that many of us are familiar with.

So when I got into ministry, all I knew was that I was following a clear calling from God to plant a church and preach the gospel. I didn't know a thing about the importance of establishing healthy bylaws and a biblical church leadership structure. I just "copied and pasted" the structure that I had seen modeled growing up...literally! I took my sending church's constitution and bylaws, and except for a few tweaks and minor modifications, adopted it as the governing structure for the newly planted church I had been called to lead. And there it was in our bylaws: voting, committees, quorums, *rights* of the membership, percentages of the votes required to "win" an issue, all with *Robert's Rules of Order* to be our faithful guide through the political fun! And early on in the life of our church, thanks to an extremely ungodly family who happened to become "members" of our church, I found myself at the center of some pretty discouraging and terrifying business meetings. I'm not so sure these people were truly even born-again followers of Jesus Christ, but there they were with just as much "voting power" as I had when it came to the direction of our church. Never mind the fact that God had called *me* to leave my career and move hundreds of miles away from home to plant this church. Never mind that *I* was the one who went to bed each night with the weight of leadership for this new church on my chest. Never mind that *I* was the one on my knees before God seeking His will and direction for this church. But these people had just as much "power" to affect the outcomes of decisions that needed to be made for our church as I did. Ridiculous!

A few years ago, as God was lighting a fire in my heart with a fresh vision of reproducing our church into multiple rural communities through a multi-site strategy, He also brought me into contact with several pastors and church leaders of much larger and healthier churches with leadership structures that were much more biblical than ours at the time. God used them to influence my thinking and help me see the need to adopt a more biblical model for church leadership before we launched out into multiple locations spread out across different counties, states, and even countries. Over a six-month process and through a series of meetings, I patiently and carefully led our membership to adopt a brand new set of bylaws in which our members would never cast another vote to determine church leadership decisions. Instead, those decisions would be made by the Lead Pastor (me) along with a Leadership Team made up of a handful of godly men and advisors. I will never forget the night that our people took their final (and unanimous) vote ever in the life of our church, thus adopting the new bylaws, which ushered in a much more biblical, pastor-led structure of church leadership.

If you are a pastor reading this book, I can't encourage you enough to prayerfully and carefully consider guiding your congregation through a similar process. Let me offer a few reasons why I believe the standard "congregational-led" form of church government should be abandoned and a "pastor-led" model adopted.

1. **Congregational led church government is not biblical.**

I've stated this fact several times already, but just in case I haven't been clear enough I will say it again. *Nowhere* in Scripture do we see the local church governing itself the way we see so many churches doing so today. There's not one mention of voting, committees, quorums, Parliamentary procedure, or political posturing of any kind in the New Testament. Instead we clearly see that God has called and equipped certain people to lead His church and He calls everyone else to submit to that leadership.

Hebrews 13:17 says, "Have confidence in your (spiritual) leaders and submit to their authority, because they keep watch over you as those who must give an account. Do this so that their work will be a joy, not a burden, for that would be of no benefit to you."

2. Congregational led church government invites division into the church.

Any time a decision is put up for a vote, the stage has been set for there to be "winners" and "losers". When all that is needed for a decision to be made is the majority vote of the congregation, the door is wide open for people to begin their political posturing and maneuvering in an attempt to line up the needed votes. This atmosphere encourages those who seek power and control to go to whatever lengths necessary to see their agenda accomplished in the church. At the end of the day, the church will be controlled by whoever has the most political clout. (Sounds a lot like Congress doesn't it?)

3. Congregational led church government is the downfall of many pastors.

I once read a statistic that said the average pastor switches churches every 2-3 years. I've also heard it said that thousands of pastors quit the ministry altogether every year deflated, discouraged, defeated, burned out. While there may be many factors that play into these grim statistics, I believe one major cause for pastoral discouragement is the lack of ability for the average pastor to lead his church as God is directing him to do so. The pastor who has been called and equipped by God to lead the church is so often at the mercy of the "church boss" or "power brokers" in the congregation who may or may not be actively walking with the Lord. Sadly, it seems the latter is more often the case. The direction of the church gets determined by men and women who not only have NOT been *called* by God to lead the church, but they're not even cultivating a growing relationship with Him. I believe a pastor can only tolerate so much of this dysfunction before he seeks relief from the daily oppression. After multiple failed attempts at finding a healthier climate in a different church, the pastor resigns from ministry altogether.

4. Congregational led church government impedes the church from taking decisive and timely action.

When we model our churches to operate based on a system of human government (i.e. Parliament or the United States Congress) we shouldn't be surprised when the church functions about as efficiently as these sluggish and cumbersome institutions. In case you're not aware of it, the bigger and more complicated a government gets, the slower it makes decisions and it operates with far less efficiency. Historically, the church is very slow to accept change or strike out in a new direction. I believe this is due in large part to the fact that in most churches, nothing can happen unless there is buy-in from the majority of the congregation. The problem with this is that a congregation is made up of *people*. And people naturally resist change instead of embracing it. Therefore, protecting status quo becomes the preferred posture of the average congregation, leaving the average pastor frustrated with the amount of time and emotional energy that must go into the smallest of changes and the snail-paced rate at which those decisions are made. Instead of being quick and agile, the average church is S-L-O-W and lethargic. Although our culture changes daily and thus requires ever-changing methods to reach people with the gospel, the average church is unable to make the adjustments needed because every decision gets tied up and weighed down in the political process.

5. **Congregational led church government often fails to make the hard and unpopular decisions.**

When it comes to leadership, there are times when *hard* decisions have to be made. Pastors often find themselves in situations that call for the *right* decision to be made, even though they know it will not necessarily be a *popular* decision. Sometimes shepherds have to make decisions for the well being of the flock, even if the flock doesn't like it. But when the shepherd is at the mercy of the majority vote of the flock, things can get ugly real fast in a situation where he chooses that which is *biblically* correct but not *politically* correct. Many a pastor has been threatened and bullied into submission by their congregation when considering making a hard, but correct decision. Many more have actually lost their job when they had the courage to stand up against the "power brokers" and "church bosses" and make the hard decisions. This should not be the case! I've heard Pastor Ed Young Jr. say, *"Most churches are structured in such a way that protect the wolves and expose the shepherds."* In order for a church to be healthy, I believe pastors need a structure of leadership in place that actually frees them up to do what leaders do...lead!

Are leaders really necessary in the church?

If we can recognize the need for clear and decisive leadership in the fire service where we are fighting physical fires and attempting to rescue physical lives, why can't we understand how much *more* strong leadership is needed when it comes to carrying out the mission of the church...fighting the fires of hell and rescuing souls for all eternity?

Recently I was talking about this very subject on my weekly podcast for rural pastors (you can find it at SmallTownBigChurch.com). I made the statement that if you were to ask the average church attender who the leader of their local church was, they would likely point to someone *other* than the pastor! I was a little surprised (although I shouldn't be considering the sad state of many leaderless churches today) by the feedback I received from pastors in different groups on social media.

I had pastors saying things like, *"Shouldn't we be pointing our people to Jesus as their leader instead of trying to take that mantle upon ourselves?"* *"Shouldn't everyone be growing to be more like Christ and therefore everyone in the church should be worth following?"*

Ridiculous!

Obviously, YES, Jesus Christ is the head of his church! We all get that! I'm not disputing that in any way. But to claim that God doesn't advance His kingdom through the leadership of called, anointed, and gifted leaders is to ignore countless stories and commands in Scripture. A better question would be why do pastors want to shirk the mantle of leadership that their office requires instead of embrace it? Pastor, if God has truly called you to pastor a local church, He has called you to LEAD! If you are uncomfortable with the weight and responsibility that leadership requires, then I would strongly question whether or not you've truly been called by God to serve in a lead/senior pastor role. This life is too short, and hell is too hot, and eternity is too long to allow the mission of the church to suffer due to lack of strong leadership!

Furthermore, strong pastoral leadership will be absolutely essential if a church is going to pursue a **compelling, God-given vision. I believe God speaks vision into the church through the life of the leader. So with a healthy leadership structure in place, let's talk about vision!**

CHAPTER 6

SPEAK A COMPELLING VISION

The fire service calls people into something bigger than themselves...

As we learned in chapter 4, the fire service is clear on it's mission: *saving lives and protecting property.* At the risk of stating the obvious, let me point out the fact that in order to fulfill its mission it will require that firefighters step into situations in which people's lives or property are in *DANGER!* Imagine a job description that includes among other things:

- Running into burning buildings while others are running out.
- Being exposed to toxic carcinogens on a regular basis.
- Operating at the scene of a car crash with traffic flying by all around, with drivers paying more attention to gawking at the scene than the road! (By the way, if you're one of those drivers...STOP IT!)
- Climbing an areal ladder 125 feet into the air.

- Performing a water rescue in dangerous, swift-moving water.
- Working at great heights on a high-angle rescue team.
- Fighting claustrophobia during a confined space rescue operation.
- Responding to a hazardous materials spill or leak.
- Operating heavy and dangerous tools that have the power to maim or kill.

Who would sign up for something like that? The truth is...a whole bunch of people would. Every year people line up to go through the rigorous application and testing processes of fire departments all across the country. Why? Because the fire service casts a vision that calls out the best in people. It invites people to give themselves to something that is bigger and greater than themselves. When called to the high vision of saving lives, firefighters are willing to put themselves in harms way and even pay the ultimate price of laying down their life for their fellow man.

Well as much as I believe in and am committed to the fire service's vision of saving physical lives and protecting physical property, I just happen to believe that God has an even GREATER vision for His church as we have been called to battle the forces of darkness and snatch others from the flames of hell for all eternity!

What if...

- What if God really wanted to do something BIG in your small town?

- What if God isn't turned off or unimpressed with the small number on the population sign on the edge of your rural community?
- What if God wanted to use your small church to make a huge impact in your region?
- What if God desired to use your small platform to rescue thousands of rural people for eternity?
- What if all God is looking for is a leader willing to ask Him and believe Him for a huge vision?

I believe a compelling vision will combat the feeling of insignificance that so many small town pastors and churches struggle with. When you fail to realize that God desires to do BIG things even in small places, it causes you to wish you were in a big place so that you can be a part of something big too. But when you come to the realization that God has a BIG vision even for your small-town or rural church, your focus will shift from wishing you could move to a bigger place to actively begin pursuing all the God-sized possibilities. You will begin to dream of ways to *REACH* your community, rather than *ESCAPE* it!

In the pages to follow, I want to share ten things every leader needs to know about vision.

1. God is the giver of vision.

Simply put, if you don't have a vision for your church, you need to ask God to give you one. I really believe there is no one more concerned with you knowing and following God's will for your life than God himself! I

would contend that if you are faithful to ask God for a
clear and specific vision regarding His will for how your
church should make an impact for His eternal kingdom,
He will be faithful to deliver. I can tell you that the times
when I have really heard a direct word from the Lord in
regards to vision have often come during seasons of
prayer and fasting. I don't know why fasting is such a
powerful connection to the voice of God, but it seems
that God speaks to me when I do it. And I should clarify
what I mean when I talk about "hearing a direct word
from the Lord," as that is often an overused Christian
cliché. For me, when God has breathed vision into my
heart and mind, it hasn't come from a direct, audible
voice. If that's ever happened for you I think that's
awesome and to be honest, I'm a little jealous! But I have
learned to discern God's "voice of vision" in the form of
what I call little mental "snapshots". That's it. I can
point to times when God will impress a brief picture of a
preferred future in my mind and give me the peace and
conviction that He is inviting me to believe Him for that
future and begin to lead others in that direction. I don't
know if that's exactly how God will give you His vision
for your church, but I absolutely believe that regardless of
how He will do it, He WILL do it. Just ask Him!

2. A God-given vision will be much bigger than you!

If your vision does not seem somewhat intimidating and
far beyond your reach, I would suggest it's not from God.
When God breathes a vision into your spirit, at first that
vision will exceed your competency. It will most likely
require people, talents, and resources that you don't

currently have. In other words, a God-given vision will be impossible without God. And that is where the adventure begins. That is where the flames of faith are ignited. God invites us to be a part of something that we can't accomplish on our own.

3. God often gives the vision before He gives the resources to accomplish it.

Money usually follows vision. It rarely happens the other way around. In most cases, God gives us the vision before we realize the resources to see that vision become a reality.

One time I heard a pastor tell another group of pastors that he doesn't need to talk about money in his church because his church has plenty of it. Whether he realizes it or not, that pastor told me two things in that statement: First of all, my BS detector heard him really say that he's afraid to address the subject of money in his church for fear of who might be offended by it. (By the way, experience has taught me that the only people who get mad when I preach God's word on the subject of biblical generosity are those who aren't giving a blessed thing to the church in the first place! So pastor, don't hesitate to call people to be the givers that God commands us to be.) Secondly, I heard him saying in other words that his church did not have a vision from God because they had all the money they needed.

Personally, I have never met a leader or a church that was pursuing a compelling vision who had all the money to do what God has placed in their hearts to do. Pastor, if God has given you a vision beyond your resources, you are in the sweet spot! Believe Him to bring the resources as you begin to take deliberate steps of action and obedience in the direction of that vision.

And as long as we're on the subject of money, refuse to let your budget determine your vision. Don't let your finance team speak heavily into your vision. They will be tempted to focus on the limited resources that the budget currently allows. Instead, your vision should scare the crap out of your finance team and keep them awake in bed at night wondering how in the world God is going to provide! But that's the whole point. Instead of focusing on your limited abilities and financial means, focus on God's unlimited ability to provide.

4. A God-given vision will take you far beyond your comfort zone.

Any vision worth pursing will demand sacrifice, risk, leading into the unknown and stepping out in faith without a guarantee of success. Needless to say, this is not going to be comfortable. But nowhere in Scripture have I ever read where God laid out a plan of how He was going to use someone in a significant way for His kingdom, and then assured them that it would be easy and would not require much from them. Instead, it seems that most of the time God leads His people out to the edge of what seems possible, comfortable, and reasonable. This is where faith is developed. This is where people grow. This is where we learn to stop leaning on our own strengths and talents and recognize how insufficient we are. That in turn causes us to lean into Christ and trust Him. It's not easy. It's not comfortable. But in the end, it is SO worth it!

5. A God-ordained vision always creates more questions than answers.

One of the reasons that a God-given vision is so uncomfortable is because we have a pretty clear picture in our mind of the *"what,"* but when it comes to the *"how,"* we truly have no clue.

- How will we afford…? (I don't know.)
- When will we know the time right to…? (I don't know.)
- Where will we find the leaders to…? (I don't know.)
- How will that work…? (I don't know.)
- What about…? (I don't know.)

As I was getting started in my pastoral career, an older pastor friend gave me some good advice. He told me to never be afraid of using the powerful three-word phrase, "I don't know." As leaders, we're often tempted to posture ourselves in such a way as to fool our people into thinking that we have all the answers. But admitting we don't know everything can be very liberating. In some ways, it takes the pressure off of us to have it all figured out and it helps point our people to rely on the God whom we serve in the first place. If you are going to call your people to embrace a compelling vision I guarantee you'll find yourself saying, "I don't know" a lot…and that's ok.

6. A God-given vision will draw people in and repel others at the same time.

So far I've been making the case that when you speak a compelling vision it will draw people to your church because people want to be a part of something that is bigger than themselves. And while that is true, the opposite can also be true as well. If you have the courage to lead your church in the direction of a God-given vision be prepared for others to leave. I believe there are some reasons for this:

- A God-given vision is uncomfortable. (We've already talked about this above.)
- A God-given vision embraces change that will lead us into a future that will look different than our present. And while most church people say they're willing to do whatever it takes to reach people for Christ, what they usually mean is that they're willing to do whatever it takes as long as it doesn't require any change.
- A God-given vision will compel us to be *others*-focused as opposed to *self*-focused. As our church has grown I have actually had people leave and tell me they liked it better when we were smaller and everyone knew everyone. Essentially they were self-focused. They had no problem that our church had reached out and embraced *them*, but they were unwilling to keep reaching out and embracing *others*.
- A God-given vision can draw criticism and accusations of being arrogant or cocky. I don't know what it is about human nature that causes some people to criticize and accuse others who

are seeking growth and excellence in their lives. If you have the courage and confidence to boldly speak and pursue a God-given vision don't be surprised when some people accuse you of being prideful.

Since it's possible for a compelling vision to repel people, let me offer you a word of caution. Be careful not to go public with your vision too early. Make sure you've truly heard from the Lord and have a clear picture of what He's calling you to. Make sure you've communicated that vision to a small group of your inner circle, staff, and key leaders. Just know that the minute you go public with your vision you will need to be prepared for the unintended consequences of the cynical critique from some and the flat out rejection from others. The world can be hard on a vision, so make sure it's healthy before subjecting it to these negative elements too early in the process.

7. A God-given vision requires stubborn determination.

Once you've gone public with a God-given vision, be ready to be in it for the long haul. As a leader you will need to have steadfast determination to see the vision become a reality. And while you should be stubborn about the vision itself, I challenge you to be quite flexible with your plan of how it's actually accomplished. God might surprise you with the *path* that He chooses to take you on, the amount of *time* it will take to accomplish His vision, and the *people* He chooses to use along the way. Regardless of the ups and downs, however, as the leader you will need to hold tightly to the vision that God has spoken into your heart. And know from the start that no one will be more excited about the vision than you are as the leader. You have to be the constant cheerleader and promoter of the vision that God has called you to.

8. A God-given vision requires an environment of unity to thrive.

As I stated above, a God-given vision has all the elements necessary to draw criticism from others. Simply put, vision will die in a toxic culture of division, disloyalty, and disunity. Pastor, if the climate of your church is not one of unity where the people are willing to get under God-called leadership (see Chapter 5) you have one of two options as far as I see it:

Option #1: Change the culture.

This will require you hitting the issues head on with wisdom, discernment, courage, and firmness. It could be that you're going to have to have that showdown with that individual or family or group of families that are standing in the way of you leading the church where God has called you to lead it. As long as there are individuals or groups committed to sewing the seeds of discord in your church, the vision that God has called you to will be in great jeopardy. Those people must be dealt with so that unity and a teachable spirit can reign in your church. That unity is the healthy soil in which a God-given vision can flourish. If you're unable to change the culture, I only see one other good option...

Option #2: Leave.

I know this sounds harsh. And PLEASE don't use this as permission to jump ship out of your church just because the "honeymoon is over" and the "newness has worn off". I don't say this lightly or flippantly. Choosing to walk away from a church is a HUGE deal. But if you as a leader are unable to bring about a change in the culture from one of division to one of unity, there is little hope that you will be able to get any traction toward accomplishing a God-given vision. In my opinion, this life is too short for me to waste my time, talent, and treasure trying to lead a group of carnal Christians who have no desire to be a part of something awesome that God is calling them to. I'll go find a team that wants in on the action. Sadly, I believe many pastors today are choosing a third and lousy option. They stay in a toxic environment and settle for less than what God has called them to. Not me. I'm out!

9. A God-given vision will help you say no to "good things" that would otherwise distract you from God's "best things".

I've heard it said that often the *good* is the enemy of the *best*. When we are not clear on our mission (see Chapter 4) and lack a compelling vision for our church, it's easy to get caught up in the distraction of "good ideas". And while there's nothing inherently wrong about a good idea, if it's not what God has called us to (a God idea) that good idea can distract us from what matters most and cause us to waste time, energy, focus, and resources in something less than God's best for our life and church. But having a clear and compelling vision will help us dial in with laser-like focus and intensity on pursuing only those activities and goals that are most important. We see this modeled in the life of Nehemiah. Remember when his enemies were trying to distract him (really they wanted to kill him) by getting him to come down off the wall he was repairing for a meeting? (Maybe this is where the term "death by meeting" came from?) Anyway, I love his response to those who sought to derail the progress that was happening. *"I am carrying on a great project and cannot go down. Why should the work stop while I leave it and go down to you?"* (Nehemiah 6:3) Pastor, when you lack a God-given vision for your church, you'll find yourself "leaving the wall of what matters" to attend to so many lesser things.

10. Vision leaks, so speak it often!

If you've gotten everything else I've said up to this point about a God-given vision, but fail to grasp this last statement you're going to be frustrated. The reality is no matter how awesome and compelling your vision is, people will soon lose sight of that vision. It's not that they're bad or that they don't love God. It's just that they're…people. They have families, work, kids in sports, financial pressures, social activities, and so many other things competing for their time and attention. If you think that you can just share your vision once in a sermon or in a letter that goes out to your congregation and then ride the wave of momentum for years to come, you're about to be in for a hard lesson. The truth is when you are getting to the point of being tired of saying your vision, you're just getting to the place where people are starting to really get it. It's at this point you will need to say it some more!

Imagine your church has a "vision bucket" and it's your job as the leader to keep it full. The only problem is that there are holes in the bottom of the bucket and so no matter how much you pour in, eventually it all leaks out. That's how vision works in an organization. Your job is to keep pouring enough vision into the tank so that it never fully runs out.

How do you do that? I would suggest finding as many ways as you can think of to drive your vision home to your people. Here are a few thoughts to get you started:

- Have a written vision statement.

I'm not talking about just copying and pasting another church's vision statement from their website and calling it yours and then doing nothing more with it. I'm talking about really wrestling with putting into simple and memorable words the picture of your church's preferred future. Get it in writing. And once it's in writing, don't just file it away to never be seen again. Find ways to constantly keep these words in front of your people.

- Post it in your building.

Find a wall where your vision can be prominently displayed in giant letters and bold font! Have your vision statement on video screens in your lobby and in the sanctuary before church begins.

- Blast it out to cyberspace!

Your vision statement should be easily found on your church's website and social media. (And if at this stage of the game you still don't have a website and active social media, you should put this book down, get right with Jesus, and decide that you're going to embrace the tools necessary to reach people in our digital age!) I'm still amazed at how S…L…O…W the church is to move into the space where more and more people are.

- Incorporate it into your new members curriculum.

Most likely your church has some path to membership that requires people learning a little about your church, your beliefs, your expectations, etc. Somewhere in that process you should be sharing your vision with prospective new members and calling them to commit their lives to pursuing that dream with you.

- "Preach your announcements."

Confession: I HATE announcements in church! It's almost like every week we say, "Hey, this is going great. The music is going well. God's Spirit seems to be present and moving. There's seem to be nice vibe and flow to our worship service. I have an idea. Let's kill all this momentum and have someone (or multiple people) get on stage and completely put everyone to sleep for the next 15 minutes with announcements!" Yuck! I realize that sometimes we simply must let people know about important events and activities in the life of our church. But here's an idea: what if instead of just sharing data and information, you connected the dots for how upcoming events help your church accomplish the vision? You look confused so I'll give you a bad example and then a good example:

Bad announcements: (information)

"This Tuesday night at 6:00 pm Gladys is in need of some volunteers to help her stock shelves at the food pantry."

"On Wednesday night at 7:00 pm we have Kids Club and we still need more helpers for that."

"There's a sign-up sheet on the back table for anyone who wants to be in a Bible study this fall."

Who's chomping at the bit to take part in all that fun? No? Well how about this...

Good announcements: (vision)

"As a church we recognize that God has called us to make an impact in our community and this Tuesday night you have an opportunity to help make a real difference in the lives of people in our town through the ministry of our local food pantry. Gladys will be leading a team of difference-makers to re-stock the shelves at 6:00 pm."

"The vision of our church is to see people come to know Jesus Christ as their Lord and Savior. This Wednesday night we get another opportunity to share Christ with 50+ children from our community during our Kids Club! Hey kids, don't forget to invite your friends from school. And to our teens and adults, how cool is it that God desires to use you in His life-saving mission! If you'd like to be on the front lines of this eternally important team, join us this Wednesday at 7:00 pm."

"Finally, it's our desire as a church to help people really grow in their walk with Christ. This fall we're kicking off 5 new Bible

studies that will help you grow deeper in God's word and connect in fellowship with others. If you'd like to get in on this opportunity for growth and friendship make sure to get signed up today at the table in the back."

Can you see the difference? It's not that the second examples are more "wordy". They're full of vision...not just information.

- Tie your vision into your offering time.

People give to vision not needs. So instead of using the offering time as the place in the worship service where we remind everyone of how bad the church's financial situation is, cast vision.

When it's time in your weekly service to worship God with an offering, instead of apologizing for receiving the offering and putting gentle disclaimers about who the offering is and isn't for, what if you connected people's giving to the vision of your church?

o Share a testimony of someone who recently accepted Christ.
o Share a video of a recent baptism.
o Share a story of life change.
o Highlight a missionary or ministry that your church supports.
o Give a recap from an outreach event that your church did last weekend.
o Highlight a ministry that is possible in your church because of people's giving.

Find ways to help people see that because of how they gave to the Lord through your church, God is using their generosity to make the vision become a reality.

- Work your vision into many sermons throughout the year.

I believe it's important to give a "vision message" at least two or three times a year. But that's not enough. In order to keep the vision tank full you will need to find ways to weave your vision into sermons on a regular basis. While all of the other ways I mentioned above are good and valid ways to keep pouring out vision in your church, I believe preaching is the number one way to keep a clear and compelling vision before your people. There are many ways of doing this. The important thing is to take every opportunity you get to connect God's Word to His vision for your church and call your people to it.

Just like a fisherman doesn't just cast one line out and leave it alone all day, so to you will need to cast vision again and again for people to embrace it and own it and give their lives to it. One telltale indicator that your church is moving forward with a clear and compelling vision will be that people are engaging their neighbors with the gospel and your church is reaching out to the community. We'll talk more about this in the next chapter.

CHAPTER 7

COVER THE COMMUNITY

The fire service is recognized as a vital source of help by the community...

As I said in the introduction to this book, if the leaders of your city decided to close down the local fire station, there would be an immediate pushback and protest of the citizens. Why? Because everyone understands that the fire department plays a vital role in the community. The fire department is ready at a moments notice to engage any emergency or need that may arise in the area where they provide "coverage".

Here's an uncomfortable question: Could the same be said about your church? If the announcement was made that your church was closing its doors for good, would there be a similar outcry of protest and sadness from people in your city or region? Or would they even notice?

Some might think the worst thing that could happen for their church would be for people to think or speak poorly of it. I disagree. I say the worst thing your community can do to your church is to ignore you or fail to recognize that you even exist! Sadly, this is where many rural churches find themselves today: overlooked and irrelevant in the eyes of their communities.

Jesus said in Matthew 5:11-16 *"Blessed are you when people insult you, persecute you and falsely say all kinds of evil against you because of me. Rejoice and be glad, because great is your reward in heaven, for in the same way they persecuted the prophets who were before you. "You are the salt of the earth. But if the salt loses its saltiness, how can it be made salty again? It is no longer good for anything, except to be thrown out and trampled underfoot. "You are the light of the world. A city built on a hill cannot be hidden. Neither do people light a lamp and put it under a bowl. Instead they put it on its stand, and it gives light to everyone in the house. In the same way, let your light shine before others, that they may see your good deeds and glorify your Father in heaven."*

I don't think Jesus is admonishing his church to be intentionally weird or antagonistic in our communities so people will say bad things about us. But I do hear him calling for his church to be so engaged in serving and "covering" our communities that people have no other choice but to sit up and take notice. In other words, I hear Jesus telling his church to **refuse to be ignored**. Christ is calling your church to be such a player in your community that people take notice…whether they like you or not…whether they agree with you or not…they still can't deny that something powerful is taking place in and through your ministry.

Let me offer some practical ways you can refuse to be ignored by your community:

1. Preach the gospel.

The gospel is good news. But it can be offensive to those who have not yet had their eyes opened to the bad news that they are lost in their sin and on their way to eternal separation from God in hell. And this includes (maybe *especially* includes) religious people!

I often say that the biggest spiritual challenge facing small, rural communities is a demonic spirit of religion that plagues its people. Unlike some places around the world where people might be militantly hostile to the gospel, rural America at first glance appears very welcoming of "Christianity". The problem is, however, that rural America has been exposed to just enough religion that so many people have been effectively immunized from the true, life-transforming power of the gospel. Don't let all the steeples and stained glass of quaint small church buildings fool you into thinking that rural America is "Christian". I have found it to be a place full of lost, religious people who when confronted with the true message of the gospel, bristle. What's the message religious people find so offensive? That their external forms of godliness and religious tradition won't save them...that they need a personal faith relationship with Jesus Christ...regardless of what denomination their grandma was...regardless of whether their parents made a decision to have them baptized as an infant...regardless of whether they were confirmed into a church as a teenager...regardless of their own self-righteousness and best moral effort...THEY need to repent and accept Christ. Don't believe me? Just start preaching the gospel in a religious community and watch how fast people begin to notice a difference from what they've heard their entire life in church!

2. Stand for God's Word!

Another way to quickly get on the radar of your rural
community is to have the boldness and audacity to preach
and uphold the Word of God…even when it flies in the
face of what our culture celebrates and embraces under
the cries of tolerance. In no way am I advocating being a
religious bully who's always looking for a fight over the
slightest doctrinal difference or practice of methodology.
Nor am I calling for red-faced, pulpit pounding, Bible
thumping preachers screaming about the fires of
damnation to a lost community. But I fear that far too
many churches, in an effort to *not* look like the guy
described above, have swung so far to the other extreme.
At best, they simply remain silent on issues to which God
has clearly spoken in His Word in an attempt not to ruffle
any feathers or upset anyone. At worst, they have
completely capitulated to a godless culture and have
embraced sin, called it good, and chastise anyone who
dares remain true to a biblical worldview.

Imagine if the fire service and emergency medical
professionals started to reject absolute truths for fear of
offending the sensitivities of some in their community.
Suppose they were called to the scene of a cardiac arrest
and were reluctant or even unwilling to begin delivering
chest compressions, defibrillation, and rescue breathing
because a growing number of people in society didn't
believe in CPR. Or imagine them rolling up on a roaring
structure fire but refusing to put water on the flames
because some crazy person in the crowd told them that
gasoline would work just as well to douse the inferno and
it was intolerant of them not to include gasoline in their
hose lines! Imagine the local authorities throwing all fire

safety codes to the wind and refusing to enforce the very laws that have reduced fire fatalities because more and more people were beginning to call the statutes narrow-minded and bigoted.

You get my point, don't you? When it comes to matters of life and death, the fire service embraces absolute truth and doesn't apologize for it. That's part of their service to the community. So why are churches afraid to do the same thing when there is even more at stake than just physical life or death? I'm not telling you to go looking for a fight. Just preach the Bible and soon enough the fight will find you! If you want to serve your community well and give them what they need, remain true to God's Word. Preach it with grace, love, and boldness.

3. Be active in reaching out to the community:

Whenever and wherever there is an emergency in your community, you can count on the fire department to show up and engage the situation. I believe the same should be true of the church. But instead of limiting the response only to emergencies (needs), I would also say any time the community is gathering for fun or celebration should be seen as an opportunity for the church to be present and add value to the event. Whether it's the local small town parade, annual festival (most small towns have something like this every year), or a school function, there are many opportunities for the rural church to be present and serve their community. In addition, your church can offer its own outreach projects and events. My prayer for your church would be for you to be so present in the community that if your doors were ever to close the community would be saddened by the loss.

4. Meet needs in the community.

For those of you who lead churches in rural communities, I've got bad news and good news. The bad news, which will come as no surprise to you, is that rural communities often suffer from a lack of resources that are more readily available in larger communities. The good news is that this creates many opportunities for the church to step into those voids to provide loving support and ministry to people in need. And while your church can't be all things to all people, you can do several things really well and add value to your community as a result.

Over the years my church has responded to needs in our community by sending out our EMT's (Extreme Ministry Teams). The following are just a handful of the ways our people have stepped up to engage the needs of our communities:

- We've done building projects on the homes of people who are unable to do the work themselves (replacing a deck, replacing a roof, etc.)
- When a huge storm rocked our community and knocked down countless trees leaving the city without power for almost an entire week, our people responded by assisting with the clean up effort as well as serving meals to others throughout the community.
- We've helped a widow by trimming trees on her rural acreage that she was unable to do herself.

- We've delivered cookies door-to-door in our community just to share the love of Jesus (By the way, Jesus prefers chocolate chip cookies and despises any cookie with raisins! Just thought you'd care to know.)
- On multiple occasions we have provided assistance to families who are moving by helping them load or unload moving trucks.
- We've served our local museum by providing manpower with a remodeling project.
- We've helped other community groups with setting up and serving at their fundraisers.
- We've painted the local food pantry and our people are regular volunteers there.
- We've served another church with a small, aging membership in our town by providing volunteers for multiple workdays when they were unable to do so.

I don't list those things to brag (and believe me, I could keep going with a much longer list) but I'm trying to point out that it's not hard to look around your community and see areas where people are in need and then respond to those needs.

5. Engage and serve the youth of the community.

If there is one sure way to add value to your community and be recognized as a church that cares, it's by serving the youngest generations in your area. While there are exceptions to this, most parents really love their children and want good things for them. And when they see a church that makes serving their children a priority, they will take notice and appreciate it. The rural church has a tremendous opportunity to provide excellent ministry to children whether as part of weekly "programming" (I don't like that word), special outreach events the church runs specifically for kids, or remembering to do something that is kid-focused at an already scheduled community event as mentioned above. It could be through providing an after-school program, a pre-school, or a day care. Regardless of how you do it, if your church makes the kids of the community a priority, people will notice.

6. Teach and model biblical generosity.

One of the things I love about my church, and consequently one thing that has caused others to pay attention to our church in our communities, is that we are a very generous church. The following are just a few examples of how we've shared our resources with others:

- We hosted a Local Heroes Banquet in which we served a nice meal to the families of our various police, fire, and EMS personnel and presented each department with a plaque of appreciation.
- We hosted a Teacher Appreciation event in which all the teachers in our school were invited to an after-school program where food was served and each teacher was given a gift bag full of goodies.
- One year leading up to Easter Sunday we had a give-away to our community each day of the week.
  - o Monday = Free oil changes at a local mechanic's garage

- o Tuesday = Free car washes
- o Wednesday = Free root beer floats handed out at a busy intersection
- o Thursday = Free sandwiches at our local Subway
- o Friday = Free gift cards at our local grocery store
- We've offered free movie nights at our local theatre in which the only price for admission is a donated food item for our local food pantry.
- We've provided free family Christmas photo sessions for needy families.
- We've hosted a free Christmas banquet for needy families where we've served a nice catered meal and given presents to all the children in attendance.
- We've given away free lunches at our city pool in the summer time.
- We've hosted multiple free will donation rummages where we simply invite people to take what they need.
- We've handed out free turkeys at Thanksgiving to families in need.
- There have been times where we have given away an entire Sunday offerings to certain needs within our communities.

All the ministry (and so much more) that I mentioned above has been delivered to our communities for FREE! To be clear, I'm not saying it has been free for *us* to provide that ministry. Quite on the contrary, it has come at a great cost to our church to show the love of Christ in those tangible ways. But we choose not to charge our communities for the ministry that we offer. Can I share one of my pet peeves with you? Something I have noticed in all my years in and around the rural landscape is that for many churches, what little "outreach" they actually do in the community is nothing more than a fundraiser for their church. Whether it's through bake sales, car washes, annual chicken dinners, or fall bazaars (I'm not actually sure what happens at a bazaar), the end goal is to raise money for the church. And while I suppose it's not a sin to do that, there is just something that doesn't sit right with me when the church is going to the very community Christ has called us to reach and asking *them* to fund the mission!

But when a church extends a hand of generosity to its community with no strings attached, people notice. It begs the question, "Why would your church do all this for free?" And that is the perfect opportunity to reply, "We believe we have a message so important to share with our community (the gospel) that we are willing to go to great lengths to earn the opportunity to share it." And while some people will be appreciative of your church's generosity, others will malign it. But remember we said that's still not a bad thing if people are talking about your church. It has amazed me over the years to hear a rumor spread around our community about our church that we require our members to present their yearly W-2's so we can force them to give a percentage of their income to our church! And as crazy as that is, the even crazier thing is there are people who actually *believe* this nonsense! You see, when a church truly models authentic generosity it forces people to grapple with the questions of "WHY" and "HOW". *Why do you do it? How do you do it?*

So how does our church get all our money? How are we able to model such generosity to our community? That's where the part about *teaching* biblical generosity comes in. If you're going to be able to *model* generosity to your community, you're going to have to start by *teaching* generosity to your people. Sadly, many pastors shy away from ever preaching on the subject of giving and pretty much avoid the subject of money at all cost (pun intended). They preach other portions of Scripture with authority and conviction, but because they're afraid to offend those who have made money their god, they just don't go there. Let me share two things with you that you may not be aware of: First of all, most people don't get that offended when a pastor teaches on money and giving provided that you deliver it in a non-tacky way (ie requiring people to submit their W-2's)! Secondly, the ones who do get offended by what God's Word has to say on the subject of giving aren't giving a blessed thing to the Lord in the first place! Stop worrying about offending people who aren't contributing to begin with. I know there are disagreements in the Christian community about whether tithing is a biblical mandate or not. But regardless of where you land on that question, clearly Scripture calls us to give faithfully, cheerfully, proportionately to our incomes, and at times, sacrificially to God and others. There's no getting around it. Personally, I believe and it is the position of our church that tithing is the starting point for biblical generosity and we consistently call our people to it. Consequently, this has allowed us to do some really cool things in our community, and for better or worse, people are talking about it! If you teach biblical generosity in your church and model it to your community, your church will be well on its way to becoming a vital and necessary part of the community.

7. Be visible in and available to the community.

Stop by any average small town or rural church at almost any given point in the week other than Sunday mornings and you will likely find a dark, "closed" building. Try calling the average small town or rural church and if there is actually an answer on the other end it's most likely the answering machine. Have you ever thought about what this communicates to the community?

When we first planted our church back in 2004, like many start-up churches we had to embrace a portable strategy, meeting in a rented community center for Sunday worship services. At the time, our church office was literally located in the basement of my house. (I'm pretty sure my neighbors thought I was unemployed and watched soap operas all day because my truck was always in the driveway during normal working hours!) So in the eyes of our community we were only visible for a few hours on Sunday mornings. Eventually I came to realize that even though we couldn't yet afford a church building of our own, we could afford to rent some office space on the main street in our downtown. Not only did this help ease some marital tension with trying to work out of my home everyday, it also made our church much more visible in the eyes of the community on a daily basis. We started to notice more people stopping in the office just to say hi, ask about our church, or seek help for any number of things. Eventually, we were able to hire a part-time and later on a full-time secretary. This helped us keep even more consistent "open" hours for our church office and also put a "gatekeeper" in place to field some of the non-urgent matters that didn't require my immediate attention. We have also always tried to be very good about responding to voicemails that come into the office after hours in a timely manner.

If your church is out of the sight of your community it will also be out of the mind of your community. Be visible. And if you're not intentional about having an open and approachable posture toward your community, you'll soon be viewed as unavailable to your community.

8. Have a strong online presence.

It still absolutely boggles my mind when I think about how S...L...O...W and often resistant the church can be when it comes to adopting and embracing new technology. I recently heard a rural pastor very reluctantly admitting that his church finally got a website! Let me be clear, if your church is just now coming around to getting a website, your problems run far deeper than anything the internet can fix! I wish that example was just a rare and random exception to the rule, but sadly so many rural churches are far behind the game when it comes to engaging their community *where* their community is rapidly spending more and more time...ONLINE! At a bare minimum, I would strongly encourage any church that is trying to be visible to its community to invest in the following areas online:

- A good website

In our day and age, long before anyone darkens the door of your church, they will have first checked you out online. And if you fail to have a presence online, or worse, have a website that is obsolete and clearly hasn't been updated in months or years, you've already communicated a lot about your church to that would-be guest. Essentially you've told them, *"Our church is out of touch. Our church is not living in the same world you're living in. Our church probably doesn't understand the things you're dealing with."* There is absolutely no excuse to resist having a simple, clean, and excellent website that allows people to safely check you out at a distance.

- Social Media

I get it. Like the internet itself, social media has contributed much evil and darkness into our world. And only time will tell what kind of effect social media will have on how humans relate to one another in the future. But I've got a secret I'd like to share with you. Social media is not going away any time soon. And it's where people are "gathering" at a growing rate. So why shouldn't the church of Jesus Christ that has been entrusted with the message of the gospel have a strong presence in that space to help bring light to the darkness? I believe for churches to ignore social media is a travesty! There are SO MANY ways for you to share the gospel, your church's vision, sermons, events, pictures, videos, stories and countless other forms of content through the power of social media. And the really cool thing is it's priced at a rate rural churches can afford...FREE!

Here are a few more tips for your church embracing social media:

- Don't feel as though you have to be on every new social media platform that comes along. Pick a few of the big ones (hear Facebook) and do them really well.

- If you're going to have it, you need to manage it and update it daily. I said it before, but it's worth restating, the only thing worse than *no* social media is outdated and unengaged social media.

- I strongly recommend staffing your church social media strategy with someone other than the pastor. Find someone (or a team of people) who are already doing a good job of managing their own personal social media profiles. These should be people who are positive and mature and have good people-skills. The last thing you want is a drama-queen overseeing your church's social media profiles!

- It's a good idea to have several people as administrators so multiple people can be watching it and respond in a timely manner to requests from the community or the occasional troublemaker who needs to have his comments removed from the site.

- You want to engage people in dialogue. It's not just about one-way communication. Find creative ways to start conversation *with* people, not just disseminate information *to* people. Be interested, not just interesting. Use your social media to listen and not just talk.

- Learn from other churches. Look around at creative ways other churches are harnessing the power of social media in their context and use some of those same principles and strategies in your context.

- Understand that social media is constantly changing. Don't rely fully on a social media platform to be your only online presence. You need some "real estate" in cyberspace that belongs to your church. View social media as extensions to the already established online platform of your website.

9. Embrace excellence.

I've heard some people in the church world say the term *"excellence"* is an outdated buzzword that comes from the church growth movement of the 1980's. I've heard those same people say the upcoming generation desires authenticity over excellence. I don't necessarily agree. If you define excellence as focusing on a polished appearance to the neglect of substance, then yes, I would agree that we're seeing a generation that longs for real transparency as opposed to plastic appearance. But I don't think that churches have to choose between embracing either authenticity OR excellence. I think a church should embrace both. Let's start by agreeing on a definition of the term:

I define excellence as "giving God my very best with the resources He's given me to work with."

Excellence is not perfection. Excellence doesn't have to cost a lot of money. But if your church is going to embrace excellence, it will require more effort. And that's exactly why many rural pastors and churches don't strive for excellence. They're lazy. Instead they embrace sloppiness and call it authenticity! If you choose to be a leader who embraces excellence, you will already be far ahead of many churches in your area. This will cause your community to see the difference and take notice. I remember having a man approach me at an outreach event our church was conducting years ago and made the following statement: *"I knew if your church was putting this event on, it was going to be done right."*

So what does it look like to embrace excellence in the rural church?

- Develop a *mindset* of excellence.

Excellence starts with the way we think and ends with what we produce for others to see. Without the right mindset you will fail to produce the right results. Question: Is God really worth our best? I know we will all answer that question correctly on paper...yes! But so often our actions don't support that we really believe that. Sadly, many rural churches have a mindset of doing just enough to get by. We bring God our second and third best and call it good enough.

- Learn to see your church through the eyes of an outsider.

Too often we become comfortable with our surroundings and stop seeing what a first-time guest sees. What do our guests see when they arrive and approach the building? What do they experience when they walk through the door? What are they seeing as they move around our building? What are they experiencing as they sit in our services? It's so easy to become accustomed and desensitized to our surroundings. Over time we stop noticing the little things like paint that is missing from the walls, holes torn in our pews or chairs, weeds in the flower beds, greeters who aren't smiling and friendly, etc. When was the last time you walked through your church with the lens of a first-time guest? What areas of your church would be viewed from an outside perspective as sloppy and second-rate?

- Value intentionality.

Can I share an embarrassing story with you? I remember one Sunday morning a few years back. It was about 10 minutes before our Sunday worship service and people were starting to fill our worship center. There was upbeat contemporary Christian music playing over the speakers to help create an atmosphere of excitement and expectation. All of a sudden that good vibe and energy was interrupted by a commercial for a national car insurance company! Talk about sloppy! Talk about embarrassing! What happened? Well, although I had clearly been intentional in communicating my desire for the kind of music I was wanting, I failed to be intentional to communicate *how* that music was to be played. Someone on our team in the back was simply playing music from an internet radio station with no thought to what songs were being played, not to mention what commercials were being played. Now this wasn't some earth-shattering problem and believe me, we fixed it by the next Sunday! But what it exposed was that I had not led our team to think intentionally about why and how we were doing what we were doing.

Why does your church do *what* you do the *way* you do it? Is it because you've intentionally thought through it and have a good reason for it? Or would you have to admit that's how it was done a long time ago and nobody's ever questioned it since. If you want to be excellent, be intentional.

- Sweat the small stuff.

Whether you're planning your weekly weekend worship service, an outreach event, or a marketing piece to go out on social media, pay attention to the little details. Often the fight for excellence is won or lost in the small things.

- Value preparation.

Did you know that our God is a God of order? He is not the Author of chaos! Like I said earlier, excellence is not perfection. I totally recognize that my team and I will make mistakes often, and I'm ok with that. We're human. But when I lose my patience and get frustrated is when those mistakes are due to a lack of preparation. I've been in many churches and watched them throwing their Sunday service together at the last minute. No thought. No planning. No intentionality. No practice. No excellence.

And before you try to insert a comment about relying on the Holy Spirit at this point, let me stop you! Why does the Holy Spirit get blamed for our lack of preparation? Why do we try to give a spiritual overtone to what others see as sloppiness? Why do we believe that the Holy Spirit only shows up in moments of chaos and confusion? Friends, please don't try to pass off your lack of preparation on the Holy Spirit! I believe the Holy Spirit is just as capable in moving our thoughts and ideas in moments of planning and preparation on Monday and Tuesday, as he is in the last-minute stuff on Sundays.

- Value change.

I will say a lot more about this in Chapter 9, but for now let me suffice it to say that resisting change is not a value the church should embrace. It's not excellent and it hinders us from accomplishing our mission.

- Go the extra mile.

Excellence usually starts where 90% of other people stop. As I already said, many churches embrace laziness and just doing the minimum over putting in the extra effort that excellence requires. Don't be that leader. Don't be that church. Go the extra mile. Often it's just that little extra touch that sets something apart as excellent. Let me offer some ideas where you can put in a little extra work in order to achieve excellence:

  o Stage design:

Did you know that you don't have to keep your stage looking exactly the same for all 52 weekends this year? With a little creativity, hard work, and a few dollars, you can give periodic updates to the aesthetics of your stage to create a visually appealing atmosphere. On my website (smalltownbigchurch.com) you can find a free resource where I share many different low-cost stage design ideas.

  o Props:

What if you enhanced your preaching from time to time with props and visual aids? Here are just a few ideas that my team and I used over the years:

- Cinder block wall – We built a broken down wall out of cinder blocks when preaching a vision series through the book of Nehemiah.
- Well – We built a well for a message on the woman at the well.
- Lion cage – I wish I was able to have a real lion in the cage, but instead we had small shih tzu (it did not belong to me!) and made the point that we often make our fears out to be bigger than what they really are.
- Doubting Doug – I borrowed a life-like manikin from Old Navy to have on stage for a series dealing with apologetics. I called him Doubting Doug and used him to represent real people who have doubts about the Christian faith. I still make it a point to see Doubting Doug when I'm in the mall and pass by Old Navy. I'm not sure if he's given his life to Christ yet!
- Life Ring – One time I borrowed a cool nautical looking life ring from a boat dealer in order to symbolize the need for people to grab onto the life-saving message of the gospel.
- Lamb – On a few occasions I've brought a live lamb on stage and described the process of the Old Testament sacrificial system and how the priests would cut the throat of innocent lambs and pour the blood out on

the altar. People get very quiet when I pull a giant knife out and hold it close to the lamb. (Don't worry. I've never actually killed any lambs on stage. Jesus took care of that for us all!)

- Jail cell – One time we built a jail cell on stage that I preached from to illustrate how our bitterness and unforgiveness keeps us locked in bondage.

Question: Do you think it was easy to build these props or go the stores to borrow the pieces? Absolutely not. It was hard work. It was going the extra mile. It was excellent.

o Coffee bar

If your church is like most churches you probably serve coffee during your worship services. And if your church is like most rural churches you probably serve that coffee in crappy 8-ounce Styrofoam cups! This is one of my personal pet peeves. Do you know what that communicates to me? It tells me you gave me the absolute cheapest cup you could find. If I'm your guest, is that all I'm worth? When was the last time you went to any nice coffee shop (or even your local gas station for that matter) and got served coffee in an 8-ounce Styrofoam cup? It doesn't cost much more money to upgrade your coffee to a little nicer cup.

And while we're on the subject of coffee, again, please don't serve me the cheapest coffee you could find. I know coffee isn't cheap, but if you're making the investment anyway, why not spend just a little more to serve your guests better?

Do you serve ice water for your guests? If so, why not consider adding some fresh fruit to the water (lemons, strawberries, blueberries, etc.)? Not only will this add beauty to the otherwise plain water, it will taste better too (not everyone at my church agrees with me on this point.)

If you think I'm being harsh or over sensitive, remember what we said earlier about sweating the small stuff. Excellence is often found in the little things.

o Bathrooms

This one doesn't need a lot of explanation. People like clean bathrooms. Make it happen. Period.

o Air fresheners

There's no excuse for your church to smell musty and stale. Pay attention to what is hitting the sniffers of people walking into your church each weekend.

o Multi-media

Often our multi-media presentations communicate far more than what's written on the screen. In addition to the actual text of Scripture, or song lyrics, or announcement information, we communicate how much time, thought, care, and skill went into the process. Don't be sloppy with what is put in front of people. If it's worth having them look at, it's worth doing right.

o Clutter

Have you ever noticed that stuff just has a way of collecting and piling up at your house? Well, the same is true in God's house too! It doesn't take long for junk to start to accumulate and begin pouring out of hidden storage spaces and taking up residence all over the church building. It's almost as if people say, *"Honey, what shall we do with our broken foosball table? I know. Let's 'donate' it to the church!"* (Gee, thanks!) By the way, why does the church always get the broken foosball table and not a nice new one? Regardless of how the junk finds its way into your church, excellence requires you to be vigilant to help that junk find a place in the dumpster or someone else's house. God doesn't want it in His!

10. Offer an excellent weekend worship experience.

I can't tell you how many times I've heard rural people say one of the reasons they hate going to church is because they get nothing out of it and have no idea what the point of the service was. They are just as confused after the service than they were before. Come on church! We can do better than this!

I'm not suggesting that you try to mimic every detail that the mega-churches are able to do in their worship services. You might not be able to roll out a 12-member worship team with a choir rocking out on a massive stage with the highest quality sound system, smoke machines, smart lights, and LED video boards creating awesome visual effects. But you can still present excellence in your worship service in the following ways:

- Have a plan for where you're taking the people.

Are you leading people intentionally to a desired destination with your worship services? Or are you just throwing some stuff together randomly at the last minute and calling it 'church'?

- Be clear.

Stop doing stuff that leaves people confused. Explain what you're doing for those who might be new to the church scene.

- Speak to both the lost and the found.

One of the dumbest questions I hear some Christians debate about is whether the church service is supposed to be geared toward saved or unsaved people. Let me clear that up for you right now. The answer is *YES*! It's both. You should conduct your weekend worship service in such a way that you are addressing both the first-time guest and the long-time member…the lost soul and the saved saint.

- Don't let your worship team suck!

If you don't have relatively talented musicians and vocalists, use canned music instead. I'm serious. We did this for a few years before God began raising up gifted musicians in our church. I would much rather hear professional music from an iPod than have to endure amateur hour with someone who couldn't carry a tune in a bucket. I am amazed at what churches allow to take place on their platforms in the name of "worship". We will let people with ZERO musical ability sing…into a microphone! *"Oh, but they have a beautiful heart,"* some will say. That may be true, but the problem is I can't hear their heart. I hear their *voice* and it's terrible. No one is appreciative of poorly performed music. Have a system in place to screen would-be vocalists and musicians. Your people will thank you.

- Plan through every element and transition of the service.

Have a plan for what is going to be said, who is going to say it, and when it's going to happen in the service. There's no reason for the leaders to all be staring at each other wondering what should happen next. Put in some effort on the front end to help the service flow smoothly without any awkward pauses.

- Provide a safe, fun place for kids.

I know I will step on a few toes with what I'm about to say. I know there are those voices that say the worship service should be for all members of the family, regardless of their age, regardless of their behavior. I'm not one of those people. Don't misunderstand me. I love kids and I don't mind putting up with a little kid noise in a church service. I also want our kids to love coming to church and feel wanted and involved. But when I'm sitting in a worship service and a baby is crying endlessly and the parents are missing this subtle cue that now would be a good time to take the little guy out of the sanctuary, or when a 3-year old is running up and down the isles being a distraction, I don't think it's cute…or "authentic". I think the enemy is likely using that audible and visual distraction as a way to interfere with people connecting with the gospel message. If you want to provide an excellent worship experience, do everyone a favor and offer age appropriate, safe, fun environments for kids so the adults can worship in a distraction-free zone.

11. Create a culture of loving community within your church.

One thing that has caused many in our community to take notice of our church is the deep and loving relationships that develop within our church family. People outside our church have even accused us of being a cult because of how dramatically some people's lives change when they get involved in the life of our church. How does this happen? Well, the easy answer is *Jesus*! And beyond that, I don't really have a simple formula to offer that will help you see similar relationships develop within your church. But I am certain of this. If the pastor and leaders of the church lead relationally and model authentic loving community in their own lives, people in the congregation will follow suit. Furthermore, Jesus will do the heavy lifting of bonding people together in the Holy Spirit (which is the part I can't fully explain). But the end result will be a church that has a strong testimony of *love* for the community to see. I remember one summer during our B3 Party (Beach, Baptisms, & Barbeque) at a nearby lake, a bystander approached someone from our church curious to find out who we were and what we were doing. When he learned we were a church he was shocked. He said, *"Wow! You're really a church? It seems like you people actually like each other!"* Based on that statement, what kind of experience would you guess that guy had growing up in church? If you want your community to take notice of your church, show them the love.

12. Have a strategy for branding and marketing.

I know what I'm about to say might be dismissed by some as being too "corporate", but I would challenge any church that is trying to get noticed by their community to have a plan for branding and marketing their church to their community. Does your church have an updated logo? Do people from the community recognize the logo when they see it? Have you ever considered printing that logo on promotional items such as T-shirts, ink pens, coffee mugs, Frisbees, etc. and getting that stuff out into circulation in the community? What about an occasional postcard mailer to all the addresses in your rural town or county? Have you considered canvasing the community with door-hanger invites to your services or events? Have you ever experimented with pay-per-click advertising on Facebook? These are just a few ways for your church to be visible in the eyes of the community.

I believe if your church applies even half of the above principles, you will be well on your way to not only being noticed by your community, but more importantly, you will be valued as a relevant and vital asset to your community. But as awesome as that is, the real work is just beginning. When more and more people begin reaching out to your church for help, you will quickly hit a wall unless you are ready to mobilize an army of servants who are equipped and ready to respond to the growing need.

CHAPTER 8

UNLEASH THE
VOLUNTEERS

The fire service utilizes many members to accomplish the mission...

If you have ever come upon the scene of a car crash or a house fire where firefighters are working to save lives, mitigate the danger, and restore the scene from chaos to order, I guarantee you have noticed that the job is not carried out by just one person. Can you imagine how ridiculous it would look to see just one fire truck arrive to the scene of an emergency with only one firefighter available to do all the work? It's unthinkable. The job is way too big for just one person. Yet when it comes executing the eternal soul-saving rescue mission of the church, it seems that often the expectation of many in the church is to sit back and watch one person do the majority of the work...the pastor!

And sadly many pastors seem to be ok with this arrangement. Recently I saw a group of rural pastors talking in a private group on Facebook about all the various roles they fulfill in their small churches. The list of weekly duties these pastors said they generally carry out was overwhelming:

- Sermon preparation and delivery for Sunday morning services
- Sermon preparation and delivery for Sunday night services
- Sermon preparation and delivery for Wednesday night services
- Preparing and delivering a weekly children's sermon
- Leading a weekly prayer meeting
- Devoting time to personal prayer for the church
- Counseling
- Hospital visitation
- In-home visitation
- Teaching a Sunday school class
- Leading the youth group
- Leading a small group/in-home Bible study
- Designing, printing, and folding bulletins
- Overseeing church finances
- Maintaining church website and social media
- Overseeing church technology issues
- Preparing for and attending regular board/committee/denominational meetings
- Janitorial duties
- Maintenance of the church building

This isn't even a complete list of all the duties these pastors mentioned, but I'm getting tired and angry just seeing all these things in writing! And can you believe that many of these pastors are bi-vocational? Somehow they're trying to fit all of this into a week in which they're working another part-time or even full-time job to make ends meet in order to provide for their family! Is it any wonder that *thousands* of pastors are leaving the ministry every year completely weary and burned out? Is it any wonder that many pastor's families come to resent the church of Jesus because of how it competed for every last ounce of time, energy, and attention from their husband/father?

And while this approach to ministry has come to be viewed as *normal* in the church, I'm here to declare it's NOT OK! Pastor, I implore you to STOP doing all (or the majority) of the work in your church! The church was not designed to operate with one person doing the lion's share of the work. This is not just my personal opinion. Let's look at a few examples from Scripture that should stand as an emancipation proclamation for the thousands of tired pastors that are completely exhausted from trying to be a one-man show:

- **Exodus 18:13-23** The next day Moses took his seat to serve as judge for the people, and they stood around him from morning till evening. When his father-in-law saw all that Moses was doing for the people, he said, "What is this you are doing for the people? Why do you alone sit as judge, while all these people stand around you from morning till evening?" Moses answered him, "Because the people come to me to seek God's will. Whenever they have a dispute, it is brought to me, and I decide between the parties and inform them of God's decrees and instructions." Moses' father-in-law replied, **"What you are doing is not good. You and these people who come to you will only wear yourselves out. The work is too heavy for you; you cannot**

handle it alone. Listen now to me and I will give you some advice, and may God be with you. You must be the people's representative before God and bring their disputes to him. Teach them his decrees and instructions, and show them the way they are to live and how they are to behave. **But select capable men from all the people**—men who fear God, trustworthy men who hate dishonest gain—and appoint them as officials over thousands, hundreds, fifties and tens. Have them serve as judges for the people at all times, but have them bring every difficult case to you; the simple cases they can decide themselves. **That will make your load lighter, because they will share it with you.** If you do this and God so commands, you will be able to stand the strain, and all these people will go home satisfied."

- **Acts 6:1-7** In those days when the number of disciples was increasing, the Hellenistic Jews among them complained against the Hebraic Jews because their widows were being overlooked in the daily distribution of food. So the Twelve gathered all the disciples together and said, "**It would not be right for us to neglect the ministry of the word of God in order to wait on tables.** Brothers and sisters, **choose seven men from among you** who are known to be full of the Spirit and wisdom. **We will turn this responsibility over to them and will give our attention to prayer and the ministry of the word.**" This proposal pleased the whole group. They chose Stephen, a man full of faith and of the Holy Spirit; also Philip, Procorus, Nicanor,

Timon, Parmenas, and Nicolas from Antioch, a convert to Judaism. They presented these men to the apostles, who prayed and laid their hands on them. So the word of God spread. The number of disciples in Jerusalem increased rapidly, and a large number of priests became obedient to the faith.

- **Ephesians 4:11-13** So Christ himself gave the apostles, the prophets, the evangelists, the pastors and teachers, to **equip his people for works of service**, so that the body of Christ may be built up until we all reach unity in the faith and in the knowledge of the Son of God and become mature, attaining to the whole measure of the fullness of Christ.

From these passages of Scripture we can clearly see several lessons:

- The principle of delegation is essential to wise and effective leadership.
- The people we lead suffer when we try to do everything ourselves. Conversely, the people and our organizations thrive when we get them off the bench and into the game.
- There are some jobs that are more important for a pastor to give his time and attention to than others. It's not a matter of being "above" performing some lowly tasks; it's a matter of staying in the lane that God called you to operate.

- A pastor's job is not to *do* all the work of ministry; a pastor's job is to equip the people to do the work of the church.

So if the Bible is pretty clear that the work of the church is not supposed to be carried out primarily by just one person, why then do we see so many pastors operating in the unbiblical model of a one-man-band? I believe the answer lies in one of three reasons:

1. It's just easier to do the work myself.

"If you want something done right, you have to do it yourself." This old adage has become the rallying cry of perfectionists and micro-managers all over the world. Practically speaking, there is some truth to this statement, but it's shortsighted thinking at best. In some ways it is easier and quicker to just do a task yourself. And you can be certain that it will get done the way you want it done. Because of this, many leaders choose to opt for the quick win and just do most of the work themselves. On the other hand it's much harder and more time consuming to identify, train, empower, and release qualified people to accomplish the same task. But in the long run, this is the necessary choice if we desire to see our churches become healthy and continually accomplish the mission.

2. It's the only road map I was given.

Another reason so many pastors accept unrealistic (and unbiblical) expectations to be the primary ministry provider in their church is simply because it's all they've ever seen or known. Essentially, this is the road map they've been given and it's the only one they have to follow. It's not like they sat down at the start of their pastoral career and thought, *"You know, I'd sure like it if I could be expected to be all things to all people in my church and work myself to the point of exhaustion and to the neglect of my family."* But that's the problem. As pastors we often jump right into our pastoral ministry doing things the way we've always seen them done, never stopping to give intentional thought whether or not there could be a better, healthier way. It's time for a different model!

3. It serves an unhealthy purpose in my life.

I would be remiss if I failed to point out one other reason that some pastors willingly take on way more than their fair share of the workload in the church. I believe that sometimes pastors are drawn towards the good work of ministry for the wrong reasons. In my years of growing up in the church I have met more than one emotionally unhealthy pastor who sought the ministry as a mechanism by which to serve his co-dependent needs. The message of the gospel attracts broken, hurting, and needy people. And that's a good thing. But when those needy people are being led by a pastor who is also emotionally unhealthy and needy, the results can be toxic. When a pastor has a Messiah complex and relishes in the strokes his ego receives by being so *needed* by others, often he will gladly take on more and more work to play the role of rescuer and deliverer to his people. If you can identify yourself in what I'm saying in this paragraph, I'm telling you that you need to get help right now! You, my friend, are headed for a crash of epic proportions that will leave a whole lot of people hurting and disillusioned.

If a pastor is doing all the work because it's just easier or because it's all he's ever known, that can be remedied with some coaching; but if a pastor is accepting an unbiblical role because of his own unsettled emotional wounds and needs, he needs to get help immediately!

Pastor, I want you to make a decision. I want you to decide today that you are no longer going to accept the unbiblical and unrealistic job description of being the primary ministry provider in your church. The job is way too big and eternity is far too long for one person to do all the work alone. You need help and Christ has provided gifts to the rest of his body to compliment the many areas where you're lacking. I want to challenge you to lean into these resources and learn to accomplish more through empowering others. **I want to challenge you to hire a staff of amazing leaders who oversee energized volunteers to do the majority of the work in your church, freeing you up to do the things you love and have been gifted by God to do.**

"But my small, rural church can barely (maybe even cannot) afford to pay me a salary! How in the world am I supposed to hire staff to oversee others?" If you're like most rural churches, the above protest is the first thing that went through your mind when you read my challenge to hire a staff, right? That sounds like a dream that is too good to be true, right? Well I want to share a story that I hope you will find encouraging, and then I want to give you a plan for how you can see that very dream become a reality in your rural church.

I was about 5 years into my pastoral career when I hit a wall. It did not take me very long of following the unbiblical, but traditionally expected pastor-does-all-the-work-by-himself-model to begin to feel the onset of burnout and recognize that something had to change. So I called a mandatory meeting of our church membership. By this time our church had grown to around 70 people. I set three different time slots for this meeting to accommodate for people's busy schedules and then told our members that they had to attend one of the meetings. I also let all our nonmembers know that they were totally welcome to come as well. When people gathered for the meeting I revealed the big news: your pastor is tired of doing all the work himself and the Bible tells me that I'm not leading you very well by playing into that traditional expectation. I apologized to my church for my poor leadership and committed that things were going to change starting right now! In the back of the room I had a table full of clipboards with sign-up sheets for a number of different ministry teams (i.e. nursery, kids, first impressions, prayer team, facility maintenance, sound, etc.). I announced to our people that as of today there would be no such thing as a non-serving member of our church. I told our members that I needed and EXPECTED them to sign up to serve on at least two volunteer teams. I also told them I did not want them signing up for too many teams either. We had plenty of people to spread the workload around and I didn't want to see one person taking on too many responsibilities.

Guess what happened next? Yep. Everyone got mad and stormed out of the church yelling something about, *"That's why we pay YOU a salary, pastor!"* Just kidding. That didn't happen at all. In fact, the opposite happened.

Our people responded in an amazing way. I believe we had 100% attendance from our members to the three meetings. Everyone stepped up and signed up to serve in a few areas of our church. People were energized, motivated, and glad to be able to help when shown the need to do so. And then we lived happily ever after, right? Well, not exactly. Although I was thrilled with the overwhelming response of support from my church family, when all the smoke settled from those three meetings I had a new problem and a new burden to contend with. All of a sudden I had about 12 volunteer teams made up of willing people, but all of the teams were being led by the same person…me! It was at this point in my ministry that a pastor friend taught me the concept of "hiring" a staff – real people, carrying real weight and overseeing real work in the church, made up entirely of volunteers.

Over the course of a few months, I identified, recruited, trained, and hired capable leaders to oversee every one of the teams that already had willing volunteers to serve in it. I created titles, job descriptions, and clearly laid out the expectations of what it meant to serve on our church's staff. The results were amazing. I watched people step up and take the weight of ministry off my shoulders and do a way better job than I had been doing in every one of those areas. I'm not exaggerating when I say that this shift has been one of the biggest and best changes I've ever made in my church. And you can make it too! In the pages to follow I will share a step-by-step plan that you can follow to experience the same freedom that I have experienced as you build a team of dedicated volunteers.

How to Hire An Awesome Staff with NO Budget

1. Decide that you're no longer going to be the primary ministry giver.

I've already harped on this one enough, so I won't go into it all again. But I will add one more thought. If you currently find yourself in the position of so many pastors where you're carrying more of the weight than you should, maybe there are external reasons you can point to or blame for this predicament. But if you're in the same situation a year or two from now, there's no one to blame but yourself. It's a leadership issue at that point. So take the first and most important step toward freedom and toward having help…DECIDE that the future is not going to look like the past. You WILL make the necessary changes to build a team and get the help you so desperately need.

2. Find the right people.

I recognize that this is often easier said than done, but I want to challenge you to believe this powerful reality: God has already provided everything you need to take your church to the next level. Let that sink in for a moment. It will change the way you look at your people and the physical resources God has already given you. So often we're tempted to look beyond what we already have and begin making a list of all the external resources we'll need if we're ever going to get to the next level. But what if God has already provided you with what you need to take another step in that direction? I believe He has. Your job is to notice them and recruit them.

So while I may not be able to tell you exactly how to recruit your prospective staff members, I can absolutely tell you one way NOT to do it. I would highly discourage you from getting up on a Sunday and publicly stating, *"Hey everyone, I am thinking about building a staff of highly motivated volunteers to take some serious weight off of my shoulders and I have openings for the following positions..."* You see, the person who is wildly waving their hands in the air yelling, *"Ooh, ooh, ooh, pick me, pick me, pick me!"* is almost always NOT the person you want for the job! So don't publicly advertise for the "open position". Instead, approach each prospective staff member one-on-one and personally recruit them.

Let me give you a few pointers on the kind of people you need to be looking for. I like how John Maxwell says that leaders should surround themselves with low-maintenance, high-producing people. These are people who do not require all kinds of relational maintenance or are prone to constant drama in their lives. They're emotionally steady and reliable. Furthermore, they're high-functioning people. You don't have to constantly be lighting a fire under their butt to keep them motivated. They're self-starters and can operate effectively without a ton of micro managing and oversight. Think about the opposite of what I just described. No doubt you can probably think of the names and faces of people in your church that would fit the description of high-maintenance, low-functioning people. It seems the very nature of the gospel draws these kinds of hurting and needy people through the doors of our churches. And while our churches can and should remain open to receive these types of individuals, there's nothing saying that we have to hire them to be on our staff and a part of our inner circle!

In addition to looking for those low-maintenance, high-functioning characteristics, you should also be looking for people who fit what Pastor Bill Hybels calls the Three C's of hiring. You need to find people who have good CHARACTER, people you sense a good CHEMISTRY with, and people who possess the COMPENTENCY to do the job for which you're hiring them. If someone has the skill set to be on your team, but they are deficient in their personal character, don't hire them. You will regret it! If someone has the skill set, but you just flat out don't care a whole lot for him or her, don't hire them. I have people in my church who I guarantee could do a great job serving on our staff but I will never hire them. Why? Because I don't enjoy being around them. They drain me emotionally. While I love them in Christ, I have no real desire to hang out with them this side of eternity and so I know they would not fit well on our team. Competency is the last "C" you look for. If the character and chemistry are there, people can often be trained and equipped to the appropriate level of competency provided that the job fits their personality and gifting.

One more thing under this heading: Since I mentioned something about personality and gifting, I would highly encourage you to have a mechanism in place in your church by which you help people discover their S.H.A.P.E. I learned this acronym from Pastor Rick Warren years ago and we have been teaching it as a class to our people to help them discover their:

- Spiritual gifts – What gift(s) has God given me to help build His church?
- Heart – What do I love to do? What am I passionate about?
- Abilities – What are my natural strengths and talents?
- Personality – How has God uniquely programmed me? (We use the DISC profile for this portion.)
- Experiences – What experiences has God used to make me who I am today?

Having a class like this in place will help you and your people identify where they best fit into the service of the church.

3. Have a clear, written job description in place that spells out the expectations.

For every staff position you hire, you need to be very clear with the prospective staff member on exactly what they are being hired to do. What is their job called? What will be expected of them? How many hours of volunteer work will they be expected to give each week? (By the way, our job descriptions call for up to 6 hours of volunteer hours in addition to the weekend worship service.) Will they be expected to attend staff meetings? If so, what percentage of meetings are they allowed to miss? The fun part about this is that you can build your ideal team precisely the way you want it. If you were able to hire people to fill any roles and positions in the church you desire, what would those be? Whatever answer you come up with, I encourage you to make a staff title and job description for that role. Once you have that in place, you're ready to sit down with the person you think would fit well into that position and have the conversation.

4. Have a clearly defined timeline for the term of service.

Since these staff roles will likely be filled by volunteers, I encourage you to put a definition on the term the staff member is expected to serve. I ask my staff for a 12-month commitment in their position. At the end of the year I have the option to either "rehire" them or tell them I'm going to give someone else a chance to serve in that role and they have the opportunity to either sign on for another year or take a graceful off ramp with no feelings of guilt as they have fulfilled their commitment. I ask my staff members to sign a form each year that says they've read and understand their job description and that they are committing to serve in their position for that year. It's really just a formality, but I think it adds a level of seriousness to the process.

5. Make the "hard sell". (Don't call them to low commitment.)

Here's another principle about recruiting the right (low-maintenance, high-producing) leaders to serve on your team. They will often already be committed and serving in other areas and organizations. It's not likely that they're just sitting around bored waiting for someone to ask them to step up and serve. So most likely when you approach them and invite them to consider serving in a critical role on your staff, you're going to have to make the hard sell. What I mean by this is don't undervalue their contribution by telling them the job isn't really that hard and anyone can do it and you just need someone with a pulse to fill a spot. That is not how to recruit high-caliber people. Instead, tell them that the work is eternally important, that it's going to require a significant amount of time and focus, and they may even need to pray about backing off of some of the other commitments in their life in order to say yes to this one. Don't say someone else's *"no"* for them. Make the hard sell and watch what happens when you call people to step up to high levels of commitment. Most of the time you will see people rise to the occasion and go farther than you ever dreamed.

6. Train them well and them meet with them regularly.

Once someone has accepted the responsibility to serve on your staff it's imperative that you train and equip them to do the job. There's nothing more frustrating than being expected to perform a duty or task without proper training. Furthermore, you will need to build some form of regular staff meetings into the rhythm of your team. In the early days of our volunteer staff, we met every Monday night. Over the years as we got better systems established and hired a few key paid staff roles, we've been able to transition from weekly to monthly meetings with our volunteer staff. It will be important for you to give them your time and attention to keep the vision in front of them and help them accomplish their jobs effectively.

Let me share one more thought at this point concerning staff meetings. I know many pastors dread going to meetings, so the thought of adding yet another meeting to your plate may sound about as exciting as your upcoming colonoscopy! But this shouldn't be the case. I believe pastors come to hate meetings for primarily one of two reasons:

One reason is that they attend *way too many* meetings in an average week. It's not uncommon for a church to have so many different committees and ministries and busyness going on from week to week, coupled with the unhealthy expectation that the pastor needs to *be* at all of these meetings. This results in a pastor who is out of the house almost every night of the week for a meeting at church. I'm telling you to shut down most of those committees and needless meetings. Your staff meeting should be one of the most important meetings you lead each week, and if done right, should help eliminate the need for almost all of those other committees and meetings.

A second reason many pastors come to loathe meetings is because the majority of their meetings are contentious and full of conflict. Most small church pastors I know dread their monthly meetings with their boards, deacons, elders, etc. I often see this in churches that are structured in such a way that the pastor is not really the one leading the church (see Chapter 5 for more on this). Your staff meetings should not be something to fear and dread. Instead, these meetings should be times of sweet fellowship, laughter, planning, and dreaming about how to best accomplish the vision God has given your church. I absolutely love meeting with my team!

7. Give them authority to make decisions.

If you are going to hire someone and give them responsibility to oversee an area of ministry in your church, you will also need to give them the authority to get the job done. They need to know that they are truly empowered to lead their teams and that you will back them up, even if you don't always love the decisions they make. This isn't to say that you can't intervene from time to time and inject your thoughts and ideas about something, but for the most part, once you've hired and trained your staff, you need to get out of their way and let them do the job you've asked them to do. I can think of many times where I have gone along with an idea or plan that one of my staff members has come up with even though I would have liked to see it done a little differently. So long as it still fits within the vision and values of what we're trying to accomplish, I'm going to thank God that I don't have to do all the work myself and let my team serve out of their own unique giftedness. Another example of a way we give our staff members authority is by providing them with a debit card that is connected to our church's checking account. They are given a budget and we have some other financial oversight built into our system, but they don't have to get permission every time they need to make a purchase for their area of ministry. They have authority to lead and make decisions. Nothing is more frustrating than being handed a responsibility, but then being handcuffed for *how* that job gets done and micromanaged at each step along the way. Don't do that to your team. Get out of their way and let them lead.

8. Appreciate them!

Most employees who show up to do their job each day have agreed to allow their employer to show appreciation in the form of a paycheck. If your rural church is like most, you won't have the financial resources to reward your staff in this way. But you can still show them how grateful you are to have them on your team in other ways. I would contend since they are serving in a volunteer capacity it is even *more* vital to be intentional about thanking them on a regular basis to help them stay energized and feeling like what they are doing is making a positive impact. The following are some ways I've shown my volunteer staff appreciation over the years:

- Thank them often in meetings.

I try to start most of our staff meetings by expressing gratitude to my team for the many ways they serve the Lord through our church. I remind them that what they are doing matters and is having an eternal impact in God's Kingdom.

- Written thank you cards.

From time to time I try to be intentional about giving my staff members a hand-written thank you card calling out specific reasons why I'm grateful to have them on my team. Some people may not feel it's necessary to be thanked with a card, but I find that others really treasure and value the personal note.

- Celebrate them publicly.

I try to brag on my staff both from the stage as a part of my sermons or on social media. I want them to hear me praising their efforts in front of others and know that their hard work is both noticed and appreciated. I really do love my team and feel honored to get to work with every one of them.

- Surprise them with gifts from time to time.

Over the years I have tried to show my appreciation to my team by surprising them with small gifts. For example, because ice cream is one on my love languages, there have been times when I had our local ice cream shop prepare enough cyclones (like a Dairy Queen blizzard) for all of my team members when they showed up for a staff meeting. One time when my team arrived for a Monday evening staff meeting on a beautiful spring day when I was certain all of us would have rather been outside, I surprised them by taking them out to the camp ground in our city park where I had a campfire going with lawn chairs set up around the fire. We held our staff meeting outside that night around the campfire. (I'm pretty sure I gave them ice cream that night too!) When we bring a new staff member on our team, we have them fill out a simple questionnaire to provide us with information like their birthday, favorite candy, favorite restaurant, favorite drink, T-shirt size, etc. This way if I want to appreciate a team member with a simple gift, I can do so by giving them something that I know they like.

- Pay for their ongoing training and development.

While we can't necessarily afford to pay salaries to all the staff we have serving on our team, we are able to afford sending them to conferences and help them receive ongoing training that is beneficial to their roles on our staff. This is a simple, but meaningful benefit that shows our staff we really do appreciate them.

- Staff Christmas Party

I try to end each year by hosting a Christmas party for all our staff and their families. We usually provide a good meal, small gifts, and have an evening of fun, laughter, and a few organized events. There have been years where we've rented out our local bowling alley and held the party there. It gives me another opportunity to say thank you to the team that has done so much to take real work off my plate and allow me to focus on doing a few things really well instead of trying to do more than my fair share of the work.

I would contend nothing of much significance in life happens as the result of one single person working in isolation. True impact comes from teamwork. You and I were created to belong to and work together as part of a bigger functioning organism called the church. Pastor, please stop doing the majority of the work of your church all by yourself. God has given you people to work with. Identify them. Recruit them. Train them. Unleash them. Then stand back in awe of the beauty that is the Body of Christ alive and functioning as it was designed to do so.

CHAPTER 9

EMBRACE THE FUTURE...BUT STILL HONOR THE PAST

The fire service continues to change, while still celebrating its rich tradition...

It only takes a brief glance into the world of firefighting to understand that the fire service takes great pride in its rich history. This is evident in the stories we tell, the characters we remember, and the relics and traditions we still value to this day. However, the mission of the fire service demands a greater focus on the future than the past.

Imagine looking out the window of your home some morning and seeing massive flames and dark grey smoke erupting from your neighbor's house. You immediately reach for your phone to call 9-1-1 to report the fire. You are anxiously waiting to hear the sounds of sirens signaling the arrival of your local fire department. But instead of hearing the wale of sirens from modern fire apparatus, you soon hear the sounds of a clanging bell and horses hooves galloping down the street, pulling a steam-powered engine from the 1800's. As the steam engine is getting ready to begin spraying water through antique leather fire hose, you notice another group of fire fighters forming a bucket brigade, handing single buckets of water down a line from the swimming pool in the back yard to the seat of the fire. The bucket brigade guys still haven't embraced the new technology of the horse-drawn steam engine because…well, *"we've always done it this way."*

Obviously this is a ridiculous scenario, right? We expect our local fire departments to embrace the changes in modern technology that make it easier, faster, and safer for them to accomplish their mission of saving lives and protecting property in our communities. And yet when it comes to the local church, so often we are satisfied fighting the eternal fires of hell using worn-out methods and strategies, maintaining a posture of resistance toward new ideas and technologies that could actually help us accomplish our mission. Sadly, rather than looking to the future with eager anticipation, for many churches, their desired future *is* their past.

Why does the church resist change?

Whether the issue is upgrading from pews to chairs in order to make a room more multi-purpose or incorporating modern technologies into the worship service (i.e. projectors, screens, video software, etc.). From adopting different styles of music to making changes in the facility. From changing service times to adding new services. From killing an outdated program to trying a new outreach event. Regardless of the change being proposed, in most rural churches there are likely one (or more) people ready to stand in the way and oppose that change. What's up with that? While this may not be an exhaustive list, let me offer eight reasons why I

believe churches are often resistant to change and what
can be done about it.

1. It's human nature.

Probably one of the biggest reasons churches resist
change is because churches are made up of *people*.
Generally speaking, human beings don't love change.
And when you gather a group of humans into a church,
the reluctance to embrace change seems to multiply. As
much as I'm giving the fire service props in this chapter
for being forward-thinking and future-focused, to be fair,
I need to admit the truth is even though the fire service
has ultimately adopted many changes over the years, it
has not been without a fight. I'm quite certain that the
vast majority of innovations that have come to the fire
service throughout the years have been met with staunch
resistance. It's been said, *"There are two things every firefighter
hates: the way things are…and change!"* I think the same thing
could be said of the average Christian in the average rural
church. We don't mind complaining about the way
things are, but we'll be the first to throw a fit if someone
suggests we do something new or different!

2. It's uncomfortable.

The truth is change is not comfortable. Change can be
awkward. Change can cause conflict. Change disrupts
the calm predictability of the status quo. And again,
because we are humans, we naturally resist moving in a
direction that takes us out of our comfort zone. I have
had people try to explain to me how they find comfort in
knowing that even though the culture around them is
changing all the time, they can rely on the timeless

traditions of their long-established church to help them feel safe and secure. Essentially, in their minds, the church is the *one* institution in our crazy culture that they can rely on *NOT* to change. I'm not so sure that's such a good thing…or a healthy thing. I believe when people buy into that line of thinking they are falling into the dilemma I will describe next.

3. We confuse temporary methods with a timeless message.

Let me be extremely clear on this next point lest you label me a heretic. I'm not for a second proposing that Christians should attempt to "water-down", soften, or change in any way the timeless *message* of God's Word in order to placate the "itching ears" (2 Timothy 4:3) of a culture that is drifting fast and far from God. I am, however, insisting that we must constantly be evaluating and changing the *methods* and tactics we employ to reach an ever-changing culture with the timeless truths of God's Word. Just like in the fire service, the mission is still the same as it has always been, but the methods of how we accomplish that mission must continually be evolving. I think it is to our shame and detriment that the church is known as one of the slowest organizations on the planet to embrace a new way of doing things.

4. The way we've been doing it has gotten us this far, right?

"If it aint broke, don't fix it." For far too long this has been the motto of the rural church. On its surface, it might make a little sense. I mean after all, if door-to-door evangelism, a bus program, Sunday School, and old

fashion tent revivals worked in my grandparents day, why shouldn't those things work in mine? However, that mindset fails to take into consideration the reality that our current culture is far different than that of our grandparent's generation. I strongly believe the church of tomorrow MUST look vastly different than the church of yesterday. You might think I'm overstating my case, so I want to double-down on that and make a prediction. Because of how rapidly our culture is changing on so many fronts, I believe in the next decade or two we will see churches fall into one of two categories (I'm speaking in very broad terms here.) In one category we will see a multitude of churches that have broken away from the *"way we've always done it"* traditional model of doing church that makes them look like just about every other church across the country. These churches will embrace many new and diverse strategies, tactics, ideas, and technologies that will help them reach and gather with people in homes, small groups, coffee shops, sporting events, online, and so much more on any given day of the week as the Body of Christ. They will specialize in reaching specific regions and niche subgroups in our culture. The second, and likely the bigger, category of churches will be those who refuse to change and are becoming increasingly disconnected and irrelevant to their communities. It breaks my heart to say this, but sadly many of those churches will be found in small towns and rural areas. If your church is just now warming up to the idea of having a website, embracing social media, or if the deacons finally approved the use of a projector in the sanctuary, I probably don't need to spell out which of the two categories you're in, right? If you don't find a way to embrace change at a much faster rate, your church's days are numbered. Let me say it again, the churches that will thrive in the future will be those that are willing to look vastly different from the church of the past.

5. Too many churches are structured for bureaucracy instead of action.

Another reason churches are often slow to adopt change is because they are often structured to operate more like the United States Congress rather than a body of believers being led by gifted and God-called leaders as we see in the New Testament. In the event that you're impressed with the speed and efficiency of our bloated government and/or you're not that interested in pursuing the example of leadership we see in the early church, feel free to ignore this part of the book. You probably have a committee meeting to get to in preparation for the big business meeting coming up in which some important votes will be cast anyway. (That last sentence is just a little passive-aggressive humor thrown in for free!) I addressed the issue of the importance of strong pastoral leadership in Chapter 5, so I won't belabor the point here. But it's worth mentioning again that structure really does matter and leaders really are necessary for a church to be healthy. Where there is a void of strong pastoral leadership, or where the leaders hands have been effectively tied through a nightmare of bureaucratic red tape, a church will naturally drift out of the current of change and find itself anchored to the rock of status quo.

6. People don't understand the WHY behind the change.

We've already seen that people don't naturally gravitate toward doing new things and changing old habits. People often don't change until the pain of staying where they are is worse than the discomfort of changing. As a leader it's important to be able to clearly articulate the 'WHY' behind any change that is being proposed. Pastors need to help the church members understand why they can't stay stuck in the status quo. Part of casting vision for a preferred future entails influencing others toward a holy discontent with the way things are at the moment, essentially helping them see that 'we can't stay here.'

7. Spiritual immaturity

Another reason many churches are so slow to embrace change is due to the spiritual immaturity of their people. The sins of pride, selfishness, and inflated egos, if allowed to have their way, will cause some to resist adopting new ways of doing things. Others will wrongly confuse their *personal preferences* with *God's prescription* for doing things and thus staunchly oppose any proposed change that is out of line with their perceived spiritual high ground. The need for control is another way that spiritual immaturity will stand in the way of change. Some people fear that when a new change is enacted they will lose their leverage of control or power within the church. And for far too many Christians, the desire to remain comfortable supersedes the urgency of the mission. Simply put, while they might give lip service to wanting to see people rescued with the gospel, they're not willing to embrace much discomfort on their part to make that happen.

8. Inconsistency of pastoral leadership

While it's true that many churches resist change due to spiritual immaturity on the part of the people, before you go and point a finger of accusation at your church members, let me challenge you to first step back and answer the following question. *How many different pastors has your church seen come and go in the last 20-30 years?* You see, I believe another reason rural churches often are slow to embrace new ways of doing things is because they know deep down that the very pastor who is so full of fresh ideas and is thus the one proposing the changes will not be around in 24-36 months to deal with the aftermath of those changes. If your church is like the average small-town rural church, they have likely seen many pastors come and go over the years. I believe that constant turnover in pastoral leadership causes people to become gun shy from jumping on board new ideas that the current pastor may have. They are still dealing with the fallout from changes that the last guy, or the guy before him brought about. In my opinion, the shorter the duration of pastoral tenure requires a longer amount of time needed to implement new ideas.

How to lead through change in the church:

Now that we've explored some reasons why change is often resisted in the rural church, let me give you a few practical pointers on how to overcome those roadblocks and lead your church to embrace new ideas.

- **Explain the WHY behind the change.**

As a leader, it is vital that you consistently bring people back to the 'WHY' behind the 'WHAT'. Make sure that they see how the proposed changes will help accomplish the mission of the church. Use vision as a shield to march forward into new and uncharted waters. Help people see how the cost of not changing is going to be more detrimental than the cost of embracing the status quo. Remind them that the importance of the mission demands that we change our tactics as the need arises.

- **Help people identify the difference between their preference and scriptural truth.**

Sometimes when people stand in the way of change, they think they are actually doing a good thing because they see themselves as defending biblical truth. It's important in these times that a leader helps people see the difference between a timeless and unchangeable truth from God's Word versus their own personal preference that is really only a matter of opinion. When possible, I think it helps to validate their preference. Let me give you an example.

Over the years I have had different people want to take me to task for why our church doesn't recite the Lord's Prayer every Sunday in our worship services or why we don't have a cross permanently on display up front as a part of our stage design. When I field questions like these, I'm careful to validate the feelings of the individuals who are presenting them. Essentially, I avoid getting into a theological argument about whether they are right or wrong to feel the way they do. I try to appreciate why they see value in such things, but then explain that we are not violating a command from Scripture by not including these traditions that mean so much to them. It's amazing how this has the power to diffuse a potential conflict. In the end, you have given them permission to still value their preferences, but at the same time you've helped them see that people aren't violating Scripture by not holding the same value as dearly.

- **Call it an experiment.**

I had a pastor friend tell me, "In my denomination, when you try something new you had better get it right the first time because you're going to be doing it this way for the next 200 years!" It seems his experience with change in the church is that once a new method or practice has been adopted, it becomes permanent very quickly. But does it really need to be this way? One of the wisest pieces of leadership advice I was ever given in ministry was to present potential changes to the church in the form of an "experiment". When you call something an experiment, it communicates that the change probably won't last forever, and if it doesn't work we can always go back to the way things were. It's not so final. It takes the pressure off of any guaranteed results and acknowledges that the proposed change may not work like we're hoping it does. I have found that even people who are slow adopters of change usually don't oppose an occasional experiment.

- **Let people know that one thing that will remain constant in your church is...CHANGE!**

I think it's a good idea to change things on a regular basis just to keep people a little bit on their toes and be comfortable with change. I'm not suggesting that leaders should just randomly go and change things for no good reason. But I'm not necessarily saying you *shouldn't* do that either! As I look back over the last 15 years that I have served as the Lead Pastor of The RESCUE Church, even I am a little amazed at how much has changed since our early days. Thinking about this makes me proud of our people who, for the most part, are willing to try new things if it means reaching more people for the kingdom. Guess what. Your church will probably go along with some new ideas as well. Work to create and cultivate a culture that embraces change.

- **Honor past faithfulness without over-emphasizing past strategies.**

I don't want all this talk about change for the future to somehow communicate that everything that is in our past is of no value. The past is important. History matters. Traditions matter. Heritage matters. In Scripture God told his people to *remember the former days of old*. I believe one way to encourage people in your church to embrace change for the future is to actually celebrate the past. But instead of celebrating yesterday's *strategies* and *methodology*, focus on the hearts and faithfulness of the past generations that caused God's kingdom to grow. Share stories that highlight the faith your church demonstrated as it purchased that old school bus and the dedication of the men and women who faithfully loved and served the neighborhood children that got on that bus every Sunday for Sunday School. Don't come to the conclusion that you need to resurrect Sunday School and a bus program. Instead implore God's people to once again step out in faith in a new direction and love and serve today's youth in a context that is more fitting with our culture.

- **Remind people that CHANGE is at the core of our message.**

At the end of the day, the whole message of the gospel is one of *transformation* in which God CHANGES us from the inside out. In order to reach people with that message, the church must be willing to put personal preference and comfort aside in order to make the changes necessary to build bridges from sinful mankind to a holy God. I've heard it said that, "For churches who refuse to change, the mortality rate is 100%!" I believe that's true. God's desire is not to see your church's effectiveness come to a grinding halt in the grave-like rut of stagnation and sameness. He longs to see your church bring His life-transforming power to this current generation and the ones to follow in the future. I'll say it again, there is too much at stake for the church in rural communities to refuse to change. Our mission demands that we push through the discomfort and embrace new ideas, strategies, and technologies to help us bring spiritual change to a lost and dying world.

CONCLUSION

If you've stuck with me all the way to the end of this book, I want to say thank you! I hope the metaphor I have tried to weave throughout these pages, applying observations from the fire service to principles necessary for a healthy church, has made sense and given you some fresh perspective. More importantly, I pray that you've been encouraged and inspired not just to *believe* God longs to do something big and awesome in your small town, but to actually take steps of *action* in that direction! I'm quite confident that wherever there is a leader and church that is committed to:

- **R**ecognizing the mission
- **E**xecuting strong leadership
- **S**peaking a compelling vision
- **C**overing their community
- **U**nleashing the volunteers
- **E**mbracing the future while still honoring the past

I believe the stage is set for God to show up in a BIG way! Like anything else however, just being inspired or encouraged or maybe having a new perspective on a few things isn't going to do much. You will have to take what you've learned here and *do* something with it. Apply it to your life and your leadership. I wish you all the best on your journey as you seek to be a part of the ongoing movement of bringing healthy churches to the rural landscape. I would love to hear how God is working in your context and be of any assistance that I can. Feel free to reach out.

Connect with Jon

I have a huge vision and passion to see healthy churches thrive in rural communities across our nation and around the world! If I can be of any assistance to you and your team as you take part in that vision, please don't hesitate to reach out to me. I would love to hear your questions, concerns, and struggles as well as share in your stories of success and triumph. Let's talk!

 jon@smalltownbigchurch.com

 smalltownbigchurch.com

 facebook.com/jon.sanders.104

 @ruralpastor

Listen to Jon's Podcast

Every week Jon shares leadership lessons from
the trenches of rural ministry on the Small Town
Big Church Podcast. You can subscribe to the
podcast on iTunes or through the Small Town
Big Church website.

APPENDIX A

I had a few people request/encourage me to share a few thoughts on the subject of multi-site in the rural context when I got around to publishing this book. While there is much more I could say about the subject, this will at least get the conversation started. If you have specific questions, feel free to reach out to me. I would love to visit with you!

Can Multi-Site Work in a Rural Context?

When people find out that I pastor a church in rural South Dakota that has had up to six multi-site locations (as of this writing we are currently at three) as well as an online iCampus, they are often quite surprised. I have a feeling if I told them our church was in Dallas or Atlanta they wouldn't think that much of it. But the thought of a small church reaching a rural context with a multi-site strategy is somewhat of an unusual concept (although that's beginning to change). Over the last decade or so we have seen many churches embrace a multi-site strategy with a lot of success. But often we see that playing out in larger churches in urban and suburban areas. We assume that for multi-site to work it needs to come from a large congregation with numerous staff, lots of money, expensive technology, and skilled people to operate that technology. Essentially, the thinking is that because of the challenge of limited resources almost all small-town and rural churches have to deal with, utilizing multi-site to reach a region beyond their small town is simply out of the question. I'm here to tell you that multi-site can and *does* work in a rural context.

So what does your rural church need in order to go multi-site? While the following is probably not an exhaustive list, I'll offer up six essentials to get you started:

You need a call from God.

While I could offer many reasons for WHY a church should consider going multi-site, I could also come up with a list of reasons for WHY NOT. At the top of that list would simply be this: If God has not called you to multi-site, tell Him thank you and keep doing church in a single location to the best of your ability. Multi-site should not be entered into just because it's trendy, or because the church down the street is doing it, or because you dream of looking into a video camera and welcoming all of your campuses to a service. Yes, multi-site offers many benefits and awesome opportunities, but it also brings a whole host of specific problems and challenges. Before jumping into the fray of multi-site, make sure you're hearing clearly from the Lord.

You need vision.

One way you will know that God is inviting you to embrace multi-site is if you have a vision that reaches beyond your single-site location. Often, God will give you the vision before you have the resources to accomplish that vision and you will find yourself with more questions than answers. I can remember standing

117

in front of my church (about 60 people at the time) back in 2009 and boldly declaring that God was going to use our church to reach thousands of people for His kingdom in rural communities through a multi-site strategy. This vision has been the fuel that has propelled our church from one location to four campuses, an online campus, and a healthy church plant as we recently transitioned what was a fifth campus to an independent church. If you're going to embrace multi-site to reach rural communities for Christ, you'll need to ask God for a huge vision and the boldness to step out to pursue that vision.

You need the right leadership structure.

I will tread lightly on this one as I recognize that this can be a hot button issue with some people in the church. But simply put, if your leadership structure is such that it requires continual committee meetings that lead to business meetings where many people get to cast votes on the direction and decisions of the church and where *Roberts Rules of Order* trumps biblical spiritual authority, multi-site will most likely end in a train wreck! I believe in order for a multi-site church to operate effectively, it will require a leadership structure where God-called leaders have the authority to do what God has called them to do...LEAD! It will not be possible for everyone to get to have a say on every decision that is made in every location. The church will need its leaders to make good decisions that are in the best interest of the entire church as it pursues its God-given vision.

You need a commitment to excellence.

I realize the term *excellence* is kind of a buzzword that came out of the church growth movement and some people are beginning to grow weary of it. But I still believe we serve an excellent God who is worthy of our very best. If it's worth doing, it's worth doing to the best of our ability. I believe excellence is simply giving God our very best with what He has given us to work with. Therefore, *excellence* doesn't have to be synonymous with *expensive*. It's holding a high standard to take what resources we do have to create the best product we possibly can. The way a rural church will do multi-site (especially when it comes to staffing and technology) will look very different from how a mega-church does it. But that doesn't mean a rural church has to come off looking sloppy and unprepared. It's totally possible for a small church with limited resources to produce an excellent worship experience in multiple locations.

You need a team.

One of the challenges (and benefits) of multi-site is that it is impossible for one pastor to accomplish alone. If you are a leader who tends to micro-manage and struggles to release responsibility and authority to others, multi-site will probably not be a good fit for you. In order to operate one church meeting in multiple locations it will absolutely demand that you learn how to identify, recruit, equip, release, and lead a team of people to carry out the vision of the church. You will most likely have to learn how to accomplish this largely through a volunteer staff in a rural context with very limited resources. (I would invite you to check out my course on how you can add staff to your rural church with a limited budget at smalltownbigchurch.com.)

You need a commitment to ongoing learning.

As I have become a student of multi-site since 2009 I have come to realize that many churches are doing multi-site in a variety of ways. There are so many creative ideas and strategies to learn from out there. Technology continues to improve and expand, offering more options at more affordable prices with each passing year. Our culture continues to change at a relentless pace. All of this change demands that as a leader you must be committed to continually growing in your knowledge and understanding of the culture you've been called to reach and the tools available to help you reach it. You will find that the way you're doing church today will not be the way you're doing church 12 months from now. A willingness to continually evaluate and adapt your methods without changing the timeless message of the gospel will be paramount to your success in multi-site.

So while I can't say for sure whether or not your rural church *should* embrace a multi-site strategy, I can say that it absolutely *can* work! And whether or not God calls you to be a single-site or multi-site church, ultimately I would challenge you to believe that the God who has called you to your small town or rural setting delights in doing BIG things in small places and He longs to use your life and leadership to make an eternal impact in your community. If you have any further questions please feel free to look me up at smalltownbigchurch.com.

Made in the USA
Middletown, DE
19 April 2019